I0338274

UNSUNG GIANTS

Who Fought to Keep Africa Free

Okoth Owity Opap

A Note from the Publisher

The publisher wishes to acknowledge and thank Dr Douglas H. Johnson for his invaluable help and support for Africa World Books and its mission of preserving and promoting African cultural and literary traditions and history. Dr Johnson and fellow historians have been instrumental in ensuring that African people remain connected to their past and their identity. Africa World Books is proud to carry on this mission.

© Okoth Owity Opap, 2020

ISBN: 978-0-6450102-2-0

All rights reserved.

No part of this publication may be reproduced, stored in a retrieval system, or transmitted, in any form, or by any means, electronic, mechanical, photocopying, recording or otherwise, without the prior permission of the publishers.

This book is sold subject to the conditions that it shall not, by way of trade or otherwise, be lent, re-sold, hired out or otherwise circulated without the publisher's prior consent in any form of binding or cover other than in which it is published and without a similar condition including the condition being imposed on the subsequent purchaser.

Cover design, typesetting and layout : Africa World Books

CONTENTS

Foreword	5
Chapter 1	9
Chapter 2	26
Chapter 3	36
Chapter 4	44
Chapter 5	54
Chapter 6	66
Chapter 7	74
Chapter 8	85
Chapter 9	95
Chapter 10	105
Chapter 11	120
Chapter 12	140
Chapter 13	143
Chapter 14	152
Dedication	171
About the Author	172
Acknowledgments	174
In-Text Citation for Personal Interviews	175
References	176

FOREWORD

As a person of African descent, I am proud to have read this enlightening and excellent book written by OKOTH OWITY OPAP. He writes this history with deep empathy for his people, the Anuak of South Sudan and Ethiopia. He begins Chapter 1 with the recent past, the Anuak defeat of the British at the Battle of Juom in 1912. Because of their organized and resilient political system, founded on kingship and community loyalty, the Anuaks outmanoeuvred the British and caused them to retreat from their land.

Following this empowering introduction, the author reveals that the Anuak of the Luo family of languages experienced thousands of years of migrations before arriving in South Sudan. Although the Anuaks are a minority society in South Sudan and Ethiopia, they are a part of a larger society, the Luos of East Africa, who live in Kenya, Tanzania, Uganda and even the Congo. According to Opap, the Luo history has been distorted and concealed due to racism. The author quotes Onyala (2019), "The Luo people built the first civilization in Ancient Egypt that spread to Europe and Asia. The Luo people who live in the Upper Nile region today in South Sudan are linked with ancient Egyptians; Anu." The author also cites the famous Senegalese historian Cheik Anta Diop. "Anu people brought civilization to the New World through writing, geometry, religion, kingship, law and science." Onyala (2019, p. 62) wrote that Menya (Menes) was the first king of the Kush kingdom. Opap demonstrates in this interesting study how the Europeans have tried to destroy the link between the Luo and ancient Egypt. Most history books that were published before the cultural revolution of the 1960s in the African diaspora depicted the ancient Egyptians as Asians rather than as Africans. Therefore, students and communities within the African diaspora were denied access to true knowledge of their ancestors' ancient past.

Because of the conquest of Egypt in the seventh century by the Arabs, Egypt today is considered an Arab state. However, Egypt traditionally and for thousands of years before its conquest, was regarded as a black African country. Egypt underwent thousands of years of conquest—by the Persians, Greeks and Romans. Ancient Egypt is deemed to be one of the first great civilizations in the world because of its contributions to writing, education, philosophy, religion, science, the arts and mathematics. Therefore, racist historians and anthropologists have systematically tried to conceal the knowledge of ancient Egypt's ancestry, the Luos of South Sudan and Ethiopia, who are the Anuaks. The author further portrays how the Anuaks who lived and reigned in ancient Egypt were conquered by the Egyptian military force led by Harmachis or Amasis. The Africans in ancient Egypt were also known as the Kushites. "Cambysis put the last indigenous king to death in 525 BC" (Onyala, 2019, 55).

The author reveals the origin of the name of the ancient Egyptian Kingdom of Meroe in Sudan. The name is linked to the Anuak language. Mer is the Anuak word for love. There is a place in Anuak land called Bur Mer which means the place of love and peace. The Anuak word Meroe or Mero means "love ourselves", which refers to building friendships and harmony in the community. It is amazing how much history the author uncovers about the Anuak people. The word Cham had been intentionally misspelled by European and non-African scholars and became Ham, Kam, Kemit, and Shem. Diop notes that Cham (Ham) is mentioned in the Bible as the ancestor of black people. We note in the Bible that the Hebrews often took refuge in Egypt when there was civil unrest or oppression. Moses, the father of the Hebrew religion, was rescued from the Nile River by an Egyptian princess and was reared to maturity in the royal Egyptian palace.

In the South Sudan government today, the Anuaks are considered a minority and, thus, do not hold major political posts. However, this study reveals that the Anuaks are the descendants of a great nation. Their religious faith and practice show their respect and support for strangers in their homelands and for humanity in general. The Anuaks should be respected for their quality and not overlooked because of their quantity. Their acquaintance with a system of kingship and government for thousands of years should prove their worthiness to be prime leaders in Africa's youngest state, the state of South Sudan. They have fought for South Sudan's independence, have endured many battles, but they have survived. This has been due to their education, moral beliefs, and contributions to civilization. The author himself is a profile in courage. He has meticulously disclosed the Anuak history from the ancient past to the present, after struggling and experiencing hardships in his life; the death of his mother and his brother Obang, who was his mentor. He has a bachelor's degree in journalism and political science and a master's degree in healthcare administration from Park University in Missouri.

Read this scholarly book by an Anuak son, who knows and can impart his society's history. He has built his study upon interviews with Anuak oral historians and renowned African Studies scholars such as, R. Collins, C.A. Diop, Evans-Prichard, S. Kevin, and S. Onyala. It has been a great honor and pleasure to have read this excellent contribution to African history and to recommend it to the reading world.

Dr Helen Chavis Othow, PhD
English and Black Studies (African, Caribbean, and African American)
University of Wisconsin
Wife of deceased Anuak Freedom Fighter,
Professor Paul Anade Othow

1

History And Political System of The Anuak People (Anywaa/Anyuak)

The Anuak people are a Luo speaking group who live in South Sudan and Ethiopia. Anuak and Shilluk (Collo) traced their common origin to Gillo Okwaa and Nyikango Okwaa (Collins, 1983). According to Anuak oral history, Gillo, Nyikango, and Dimo were brothers. They were children of King Okwaa. Collins stated that the Anuak original homeland was in Gezira, an island between the Blue Nile and White Nile during the twelfth or thirteenth centuries. The Anuak oral tradition confirmed that they came from Dongola in Northern Sudan.

History of the Luo people has been distorted and changed by European scholars to conceal the truth about their original homeland thousands of years before migrating to Southern Sudan. Without a doubt, racial discrimination had played a big role in the concealment of Luo ancient history. According to Onyala (2019), the Luo people built the first civilization in Ancient Egypt that spread to Europe and Asia. Furthermore, Diop (1989) stated that Anu people brought civilization to the new world through writing, geometry, religion, Kingship, law, and science. Similarly, Onyala (2019) asserted that Luo people made beautiful arts, invented letters, and the art of writing. The political stability in the Kush kingdom showed that Luo were advanced in human development. Onyala (2019, p. 62) wrote that Menya (Menes) was the first king of the Kush kingdom. Rwoth (king) Menya ruled the Kush kingdom and his kingship expanded into the lower Nile region which is now Egypt. He stated that when Luo people were in Egypt, strange people invaded their country from the North. Those invaders were described as white, red, brown, or yellow people (Onyala, p. 55). Therefore, Onyala found that the Luo people developed a stable kingdom with its headquarters in Napata: Grand Court at the foot of the mountain. This confirmed that the first brown people who met with the Luo people demolished the Kush kingdom and the last king was Rwoth Owing Wod Pule Rac Koma (Onyala, p. 55). Rwoth or Reth means king in Luo language.

Burying the link between Luo and ancient Egyptians was a deception strategy to deny Luo presence in Egypt, thousands or millions of years ago before their migration to South Sudan. Onyala (2019) explained that the first attempt by the Europeans was to unlink Egypt from Africa meaning that Egypt was considered an Arab state in the Middle East. It proved that Europeans were taking credit of civilization away from the real builders—the Luo people. Another strategy was to conceal the identity of the Luo who used to live in Egypt before the invasion of their country by foreigners. In the same manner, Western writers strived to hide the truth by creating confusion to make it impossible to trace civilization to the African people. For example, in the nineteenth century, African scholars tried to examine the true history of ancient Egypt, but their mission failed because colonizers blocked access to the field (Onyala, 2019). The truth meant that white supremacy of the imperialists, which was built on deception, would be discovered.

Although the African scholars knew that ancient Egyptians were black Africans, they needed to know what tribe they came from. After the independence of African states, African and non-European scholars were able to examine Egyptian history, culture, language, and artefacts to prove their real identity. Their findings restored fractured pieces of history which proved that ancient Egyptians were Luo people. To connect Luo with the ancient Egyptians, African and Luo scholars carried out extensive research that confirmed it was the Luo people or Anu who built the first human civilization from scratch. To arrive at their conclusion, they searched for evidence, archaeological artefacts, or language affinity with certain Nilotic tribes. (Diop,1981) suggested that it would be easier for the African writers to study ancient Egyptian history through linguistic affinity, names, cultural similarities, and gods to link Anu with members of their tribe in South Sudan and beyond.

This is how they found Luo people were **"Anu people."** Onyala (2019, p. 66) states that in the past, Luo people were known by different names such as Egyptians or Phoenicians. It suggested that Anu, Luo, and Phoenicians were the same people. Research confirmed the Luo invasion at Napata by mercenary groups was supported by the Egyptian military force led by Harmachis or Amasis (Onyala, p. 60). According to Onyala, the invasion occurred when the last king had been in power for two years. During his short reign, the Kush kingdom was invaded by Egyptian expeditions, which were reinforced by Greek and Carina mercenaries commanded by generals Amasis and Potasimto (Onyala, 2019). After his defeat by multiple forces of invaders, the king was killed, which marked a total defeat and collapse of the kingdom in Egypt. "Cambbysis put this last indigenous king to death in 525 BC," he revealed. King Owing Wod Pule Rac Koma was the last in the Kush kingdom, but he was executed (Onyala, p. 55).

According to Onyala, the Greek people came to worship the Luo/Egyptian gods between 250-225 BC. During that time, Luo had lost control of Egypt to the Greek people (Onyala, p. 66). After Luo was defeated, the Greek ruled Egypt and adopted the existence of civilization, political system, and indigenous culture. It is worth mentioning that Luo invented the alphabet, writing, and arts. Onyala revealed that Romans and Greeks adopted the Luo alphabet and modified them according to their languages. Overall, Luo introduced civilization not only to the Greeks, but also to the world at large, according to Diop. In other words, Europeans adopted civilization from the African people. Diop (1974) asserted that "In early times, the Luo people and the Nubians worshipped one of the gods in Egypt. This god is called Anu and the Luo have been referred to by historians and anthropologists as the true people of Anu (Itiyo-pi-Anu)." This finding proved that Luo people used to live in Egypt before their country was invaded.

However, when Egypt lost its independence to foreign rule, various things changed. For instance, examining what had changed after the Arabs and Europeans ruled Egypt for centuries, the names of Egyptian kings no longer sound like Luo names. Luo people realized that some of their names were changed, so it was no longer easy for them to recognize. Firstly, 90 per cent of Luo's names have meanings that can be understood by Luo speakers. For example, Owar is a boy who was born at night. Okello is a male born after twins. Oleny is a person born during war time. Most names of males start with the letter "O" Meanwhile the majority of female names start with the letter "A": Apiew and Achan are twin girls. Apiew means first and Achan refers to the late comer. Akach is a girl born in the time of famine. The point is that most of Luo names have meaning.

Therefore, some of their words and names found in Egyptian history were evidence of their discovery. As mentioned earlier, the first king of Egypt was called **Menya**. However, Europeans spelt his name Menes, according to Onyala. Due to the dedication of African scholars, the linguistic approach they used revealed that Luo lived in Lower Egypt prior to their migration to South Sudan. It suggested that constant wars and invasions forced them to relocate, leaving their homes. Regarding the names of Luo people, researchers found that Europeans had difficulty pronouncing Luo names that began with **"NY"** (Onyala 2019, p. 62). Names such as, Nyikango, Nyigwo, Nyang, Nyanza, Meny and so on. To pronounce those names easily, Europeans omitted NY according to Onyala. The omission of some letters created confusion because it corrupted the true meaning of Luo names. For example, King Menya, his real name was spelt differently by removing **Y**. As a result of manipulation, Menya was changed into **Mena**. Meanwhile, Diop noted the same name was also changed to **Menes**. For that reason, the meaning of the Luo name was lost. "**Menya**" in Anuak language means shine light on me or light a torch on me. Meny is commonly used when looking for something in the dark using fire or flashlight. Today, Anuak people use the word "**Menya-ki- camera**" when they ask someone to take their pictures. Diop's article, *Origin in ancient Egypt*, written in 1974, noted that in Ancient Egypt there was a word Mer, which means love in the Luo language (Onyala, 2019, p. 60). Finding Mer (love) in the history of Egypt confirmed that Luo people were the ancient Egyptians. Above all, ancient Egyptians were culturally, linguistically and ethnically, Luo people.

In Anuak land, there is a place called Bur-Mer, which means a place of love and peace! Another word is Meroe or Mero (love ourselves) which refers to building friendships and harmony in the community, according to Onyala. Through linguistic connections, names, words, cultural similarities, gods, and kingdoms, all were found in Acholi, Anuak, Pari, and Collo. It proved beyond reasonable doubt that the Luo were the first civilized people in Africa and their civilization was adopted worldwide. Diop (1974) contributed heavily to connecting Egyptian history to those of the Luo people. Through his research he found that the Meroitic state originated from the Luo people (Onyala, 2019, p. 60).

Who Were The Ancient Egyptians?

The ancient Egyptians knew their race and true history as black people. In the deception process, their names were spelled wrongly, missing certain letters, or intentionally omitted so that Luos could not recognize their own names. It is a credit to African researchers for going deeper into history. According to Diop, Egyptian origin was clear and recorded. They originated from Cham (Diop, 1989, p. 71). Cham is a popular name among Anuak people. It proved that Anuak people lived in Egypt for thousands of years before they migrated to the Upper Nile. This name is common in the royal family and for commoners alike. For example, King Akway Cham Gillo reigned from 1910 to 1920 and his son Cham-wara-Akello was crowned in 1921. Diop asserts that to confuse people about Egyptian origins, Cham was spelled in various ways to mislead Africans. Below are the ways European writers spelt Cham in their books: **Ham, Kam, Cam, Kemit,** and **Shem.** All these five names were meant to change "Cham" into something else. Their distortions of the Luo names went too far including one in the Bible. According to Diop, Ham (Cham) was the Biblical ancestor of the Black people (Diop, 1989, p. 71).

Ancient Egyptians were black Africans from the Anu or Luo tribe. In addition, the first Europeans who came to Egypt never questioned the race of the Anu people because they knew that the Anu people were black. Centuries later, after Egypt's invasion, a falsification of Egyptian race was created by the Europeans with the intention to change the origin of civilization outside of Africa, its birthplace (Diop,1989, p. 85). These were desperate attempts to whiten the founders of civilization in Egypt, according to Diop. Falsifying the history was intended to mask the identity of indigenous black people in Egypt. It was a new strategy that came into effect after Egypt lost its sovereignty but some Europeans who visited Egypt when it was a powerful kingdom confirmed that Egyptians were black people. Diop reports details of Herodotus's personal observation when he was in Egypt: "Undoubtedly the basic reason for this is that Herodotus, after relating his eyewitness account informing us that the Egyptians were blacks, then demonstrated, with rare honesty (for a Greek), that Greece borrowed from Egypt all the elements of her civilization, even the cult of the gods, and that Egypt was the cradle of civilization."

According to him, after Alexander conquered Egypt, interracial marriages between blacks and whites occurred. Crossbreeding resulted in a higher population of mixed race in the country. Due to people who were mixed race, white scholars claimed that ancient Egyptians who started civilization in Egypt were white (Diop, 1989). This notion was built on skin games to rob black people of their civilization. In fact, all Egyptian kings were black people! To promote their racial stereotype, Europeans began to hide the identity of Luo people to make them white in their history books. This means that when a person is seeking the truth about the origin of civilization, Anu people were whitened or made whites (Diop, 1989). "On the other hand, he is whitened whenever one seeks the origin of civilization, because there he is inhabiting the first civilized country in the world," Diop said.

Consequently, it showed that the falsification of Egyptian race was designed to alter blacks' achievements. During the ancient Egyptian period, Anu people were the builders of pyramids and all Egyptian civilizations. Secondly, Diop asserted that the notion of Eastern and Western Hamites was a fiction, not real people who lived in Egypt. He wondered where these people came from and what language they spoke. Lastly, it seemed unrealistic for the so-called Hamites to start civilization in another country while they could not do it in their country of origin (Diop, 1989). According to him, if any group of people were capable of doing what Egyptians did, they would have done it in their homeland. After all, Hamite/Hamitic were distorted names drawn from Cham who was an Anuak/Anu man. At this point, it was obvious that no Eastern or Western Hamites brought civilization to the Egyptian people. It was all African made without Europeans' participation.

Diop (1989) asserted that Herodotus visited Egypt after it had lost its independence to foreign invaders. Hence, it was ruled by those invaders. But each country ruled Egypt for a certain period and later another country took over and continued to rule Egypt. This was the birthplace for kingship, religious beliefs, and humanity. As the centre for ideologies that liberated humans from savagery and barbarism, Egypt became a battleground for foreigners because of its rich culture. "Conquered by Persians in 525 BC, from then on it was continually dominated by foreigners: after the Persians came, the Macedonians under Alexander (333 BC), the Romans under Julius Caesar (50 BC), the Arabs in the seventh century, the Turks in the sixteenth century, the French with Napoleon, then the English at the end of the nineteenth century," Diop said. For thousands of years before invasion, Egyptians developed monarchs that became the foundation for modern political systems worldwide. This suggests that every nation adopted Egyptian traditions: science, politics, religion, laws, and so forth. African political organizations were more advanced in the ancient times. However, in the fifteenth century when Africans and Europeans encountered one another again, some African political institutions were still superior or at least equal to those of Europe. Diop (1989, p. 23) reports that when Europeans—Portuguese, Dutch, French, and English—began trading with the people in West Africa, he said African nations had better political systems than Europeans.

He further asserted that during 7000 BC the desert dried up and Luo people migrated to where life was suitable for farming and green pastures for their cattle (Diop,1989, p. 22). Hence, some of those people who used to live in the Sahara Desert moved toward the Upper Nile region according to Diop. Giving credit to the rightful builders of civilization, it took a lot of work to prove that it was the Anu people who built the first civilized nation on earth.

Anu people are the Anuak people, but their names were spelt in various ways: Anu, Anuak, Anywaa. The Anuaks' link with the Egyptians were concealed! Anuak history traced their migrations in the following order: from Dongola to Gezira, then to the Upper Nile region. Collins (1983) reiterated that the Anuaks' original homeland was in Gezira between Blue Nile and White Nile in the twelfth or thirteenth centuries. According to him, they moved to Bahr el Ghazal and later migrated to the Upper Nile in the fifteenth century. Africans wondered why it was too difficult for the Europeans to tell the truth! Diop states that, "Henceforth, even when the proofs piled high before their eyes, the experts refused to see them except through blinkers and would always interpret them falsely."

The quotation above is meant to take readers deeper into a world of manipulation and deception. It shows that when it comes to the identity and race of ancient Egyptians, whites claimed them. Their strategy suggested that they wanted to make the white race the founders of civilization in Egypt, according to Diop. In this case, some Europeans believed that white men were the source of African civilization that began in Egypt. Ironically, when Herodotus, a Greek man who came to Egypt in the fifth century BC stated that civilization was more than 10,000 years old before the arrival of Europeans in Egypt—an African nation (Diop,1989). Although the country had changed drastically due to foreign rule, its original civilization could be traced to Anu people, the black Africans. This simple fact shocked white supremacists who tried to change black history in Egypt, a country they invaded after its civilization had already flourished. "The birth of Egyptology thus marked by the need to destroy the memory of a Negro Egypt at any costs and in all minds," Diop stated. This meant the pride of Africans to be the first humans who introduced writing and religion to the Greeks and the rest of the world, was rejected by the Europeans.

In the view of Europeans, black people were incapable of starting civilization! Without evidence to support their hypothesis, they assumed that civilization started either in Europe, or Asia, because they believed it could not start in Africa (Diop,1989). Furthermore, the attempt was racist in nature because Europeans believed that Africans played very little role in the world. They ignored that during the ancient times, Africans took a leading role in the economy, military, and technology. Thus, the Europeans started to distort and whiten world history. For that reason, white people could not accept any proof that black people were the founding fathers of civilization who brought light to the world. It started with developing kingship to secure human society. For example, political unification of the Nile inhabitants was established by Menya or Menes, the first Egyptian king, according to Diop. King Menya was a Luo man. It indicated that the first and second Egyptian dynasties began from 3000 BC to 2778 BC. (Diop, p.204). At the same time, Diop states that by the time the Third Dynasty took over from the following period (2778 BC to 2723 BC), a centralized monarchy was achieved. It took 200 years for the kingdom to reach its pinnacle. "However, it required no less than two centuries of struggle and effort to reunify Egypt in 2065 BC," Diop added. At this point, the king believed that his divine right to rule came directly from God. "He proclaimed the principle of his omnipotence by divine right and added "Great God" to his titles and was free from human control." Diop's analysis presented Egyptian history accurately and gave credit to the ancient Egyptians—the Luo people. He cited the importance of Egyptian achievements including building pyramids. They did not stop there. The ancient Egyptians brought writing, geometry, religion, and science to the entire human race, he said.

In conclusion, Egypt was the source for Greeks who pursued knowledge since the Twelfth Dynasty of the Kush kingdom. Diop (1989, P.234) asserted that ancient Egyptians were the first humans to invent mathematics, calendar, astronomy, sciences, arts, religion, agriculture, social organizations, medicine, writing and architecture. Those inventions spread to Greece and the rest of Europe. Due to its earliest civilization, Greek scholars and philosophers were taught in Egypt. After all, it proved that all famous Greek philosophers and scholars including Plato, Aristotle, Solon, Thales, Lycurgus, and Pythagoras were taught in Egypt by black people (Diop,1989, p. 232). The various influence on Greek society could not be denied. Thus, two-thirds of Greek scholars were trained in Egypt, Diop said. According to Egyptians, they educated Greek people with the intention to lift them up from backwardness and deeper barbarism. With evidence presented so far, Diop wrote: "As Egypt is a Negro country, with a civilization created by Blacks, any thesis tending to prove the contrary would have no future." (Diop, 1989).

King Menya (Menes/Mena) Founder of First Dynasty that Unified Upper and Lower Nile.

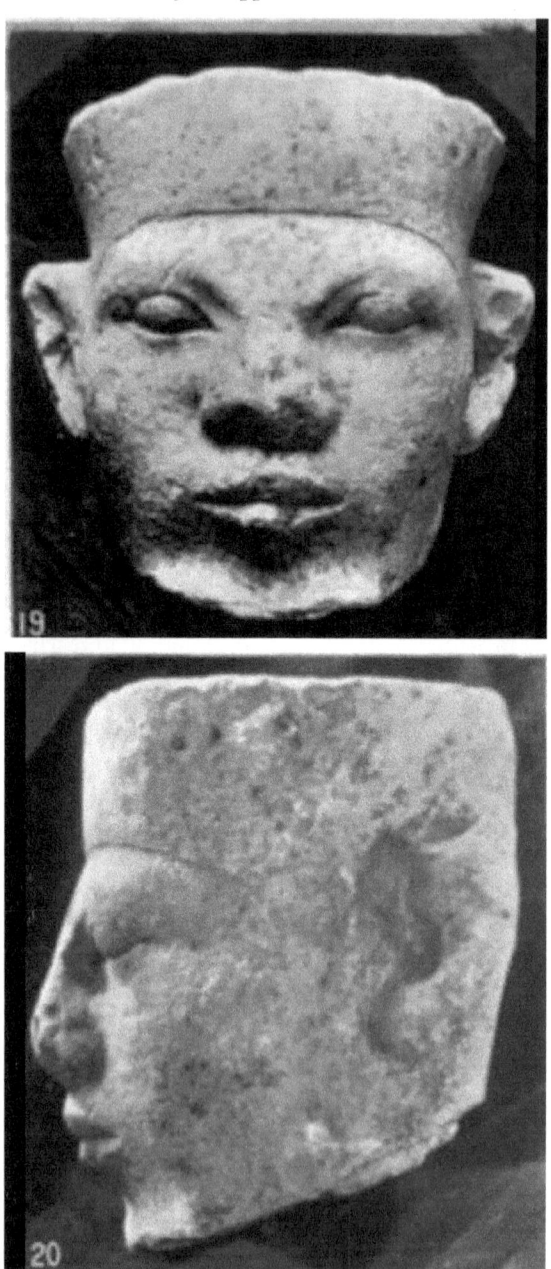

The Anuaks' Gods and Beliefs

Onyala (2019) found that Greeks worshiped the Luo/Egyptian gods between 250 BC 225 BC. The similarities between the Anuaks' gods and Egyptian gods were not a coincidence. It was the expansion of one religious' doctrine, which stretched from the Lower Nile to Upper Nile where Gillo and Nyikango built their new kingdoms. In the same manner, the Anuak believed in many gods as did their ancestors in Egypt. "The Anuak believe in an all-powerful spirit whom they called Jwok, but no particular form or place is assigned for him," Evans-Pritchard said. Each god has unique functions and rituals that require sacrification or offering at certain times at its sacred place.

Here is a sample of Anuak gods:

Jwok Nyingalabuye (Creator of earth and heaven). He is the god of blessing (Gwieth). The god of all the gods, according to Anuak people. He has the power to heal the sick and protect the nation from evil spirits and harm. Jwok Nyingalabuye is a spirit and his dwelling place is **Buc Jwok** (heaven/kingdom).

Jwok-Nyundungnu (Satan, god of curse—Acieni). He is the god that makes people sick and die. He is the god of jealousy and hatred who prevents or disturbs peace and harmony in the community.

Abella/Aballa is a god who lives at the foot of a mountain known as Tier Abella in the Tiernam region. He is known for his severe punishment when someone attempts to desecrate his sacred site or act in a disrespectful way. Desecrating Abella's site is believed to cause physical deformity of the offender. Hence, people behave respectfully and with utmost care when they approach Mount Abella.

Dingur is a god who comes to a person through the medium of a dream and his messenger delivers a message to a pregnant woman. Usually, Dingur mentions the name of a pregnant woman in the community. In his message, he informs the dreamer whether the pregnant woman will give birth to a boy or girl. He will also indicate that the baby will bear his name, Dingur, to honour him. If his message is ignored, the baby will die after birth, according to Anuak tradition. Sometimes the baby survives but will have a disability as punishment for the disobedience. Additionally, every god's name is gender neutral meaning that the name can be used for both males and females.

Nyigwo also comes in dreams instructing the dreamer that the chosen baby must bear his name.

Anyone with the name Nyigwo, Abella or Dingur is named after gods (Jwok). Nevertheless, rituals of each god are performed differently by a person who has spiritual authority to do so. A person must be a landowner or a member of a clan where a particular god resides. The spiritual man leads the prayers and offers sacrifices to the spirit of the god in that place. The Anuak people believe in the existence and spiritual power of their many gods and these principles of religion are entrenched and respected in Anuak culture.

Impact of Arab Immigrants on The Luo

In the fourteenth century, the Luo people lived in the vicinity of Rumbek in Bahr el Ghazal (Collins, 1983). Today, all Luo people remember that, once, they lived in a place called Wipacc, which meant an abandoned home in the Luo language. Moreover, they remember Wipaac as their homeland before starting another journey in the succeeding centuries. In the fifteenth century, some Luo people moved from Wipaac in Bahr el Ghazal to settle elsewhere. At this time, those Luo groups were led by two brothers, Gillo Okwaa and Nyikango Okwaa, migrating north to what is now the Upper Nile region in South Sudan. The Luo people finally settled in Malakal and Fashoda, according to Anuak oral history. While living together in those places, they called themselves Luos. This indicated that new names such as Collo and Anuak came later after Gillo and Nyikango quarrelled and separated.

Although Luo settled in Malakal permanently, another group led by Gillo Okwaa separated from the main body, migrating north and east towards the Sobat River (Openo) (Collins, 1983). These people are known today as the Anuak people. Yet, Anuak is not a new name—they are called **Anu** in Ancient Egypt, referring to their roots. It is tradition for Luo groups to name themselves differently when they formed a new society far away from the rest of the Luos. Historically, Luo was one tribe. This means when some people moved out from Malakal, they named their group differently from the rest of the Luo. For example, when Gillo and his group moved, they used "**Anuak**" after settling where they are today. Gillo Okwaa founded Paanywaa (Anuak country). Citizens from this nation are called Anuak/Anywaa. In ancient Egyptian history, Anu people were the Luos, according to Diop. Therefore, Gillo used a similar name: Anuak. The rest of the Luos who remained in Malakal under leadership of Nyikango called themselves **Collo**.

There were eleven Anuak political states/regions in their governance system—Nyium, Ciro/Akobo, Openo, Baat Gillo, Lul/Thim, Ojwa, Adongo, Nyikani, Jor, Rwanye and Tiernam (Evans-Pritchard, 1940).

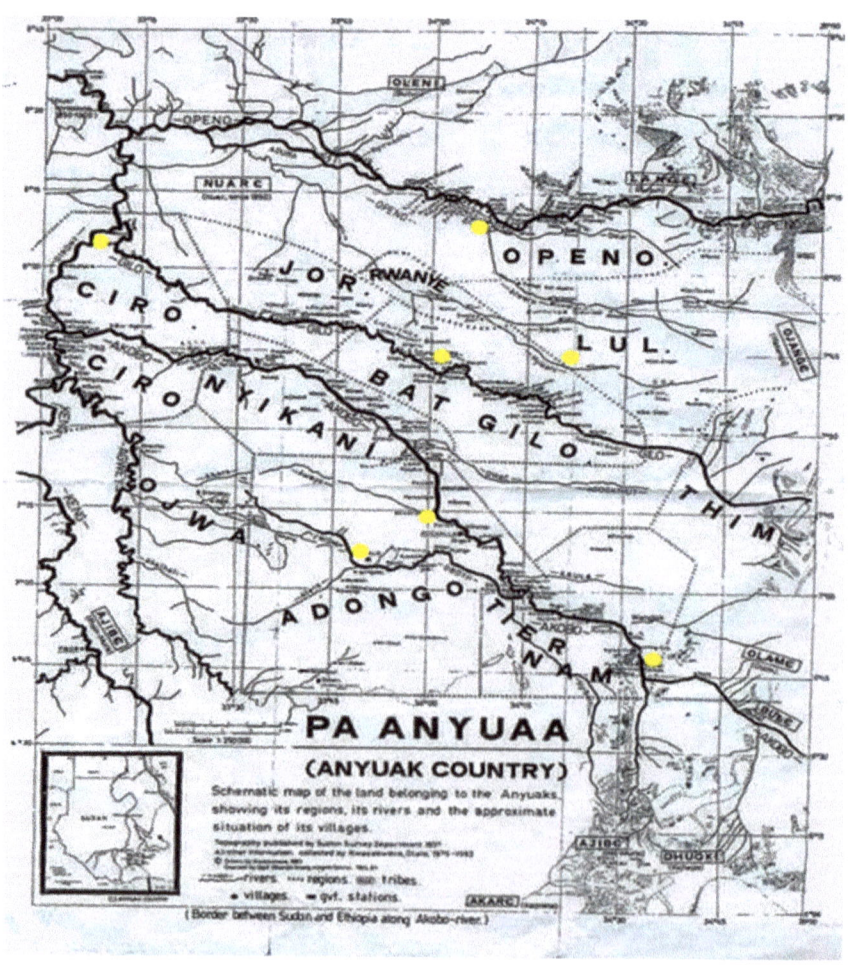

The Conflict of Two Brothers: Gillo and Nyikango

Migration of Anuak people from their previous home in Malakal was due to a brotherly dispute. Anuak oral history states that Gillo borrowed a hunting spear (Tong) from his older brother, Nyikango. The spear was given to Gillo and he went hunting with it. He speared an elephant, but it did not die on the spot. As a result, the injured elephant ran off with the spear stuck in its hide. Gillo kept chasing the elephant to kill it and retrieve the spear, but that did not happen!

When Gillo came home from hunting, he reported that the spear was taken by the injured elephant. Nyikango was not happy when Gillo told him that the ancient spear was lost—it was a blessed spear (Olaw) that was passed down from father to son in the line of the royal family for generations. It was considered the blessing spear in Luo culture. Nyikango ordered Gillo to return to where he speared the elephant and bring back the spear back, according to Anuak legend. Gillo had no choice but to retrace the footsteps of the wounded elephant to find the spear. During that long journey, Gillo was angry, tired, frustrated and pessimistic of finding the spear. An account of the Anuak people asserted that it took Gillo days to find the spear lying by the dead elephant. Gillo returned home carrying the spear and gave it to Nyikango. This incident not only created tension, but it also developed unfriendly relations between the two brothers.

According to Onyala (2019) it was not only the issue of spear but also the bead that caused division among children of Okwaa. Onyala referred to the dispute between Dimo and Nyikango. But ancient Luo history involved Nyikango in both mysteries. During their hostilities, Gillo was putting beads on a string when Nyikango's child picked up one of Gillo's beads and swallowed it. Although the baby was innocent, the dissent created by the spear incident made the child a victim because Gillo demanded the return of his bead immediately! Nyikango told him to wait until the baby passed stool and he would search for the bead in the stool. Gillo refused to wait! His impatience was meant as a retaliation for what Nyikango did to him when the wounded elephant took the spear. Finally, Nyikango decided to kill his child and opened her stomach to retrieve the swallowed bead. He gave the bead to

Gillo. This was the root cause of the separation between Gillo and Nyikango, according to Anuak history. However, after their separation, the two Luo brothers reconciled and lived in harmony in their respective Kingdoms. They are one people, culturally, historically and linguistically. Overall, both Collo and Anuak maintained the Luo kingdoms up to this day!

In the seventeenth century, another group of Anuak moved out from Ojwa state to Lafon Hill where, today, they called themselves Pari (Collins, 1983). Those people migrated from the Ojwa region in Anuak land. To be exact, Pari people left their original homeland in Ojwaan-Boy's villages in the southern part of Paanywaa. During their migration, some members of their families or clan members did not migrate with them. They remained in Ojwa state permanently. As a Luo custom, when Pari people moved from the larger group of Anuak people, they named themselves "**Pari**" following their arrival in Lafon Hill. In this case, they dropped Anuak's name completely, while naming their new group, Pari. But they maintained the Luo language and culture. When it comes to language affinity, Pari and Anuak are completely intelligible. Despite centuries since leaving the Anuak land, Anuaks still called them (**Jo-Boy**) which meant people of Boy's villages.

While Pari people were living in Lafon, another group from the Pari community moved to Parjwok. They are now called **Acholi**. About the same time, some of the Acholi people penetrated further south into northern Uganda (Collins, 1983). It clearly showed that when the Luo family migrated to different places, they used new names to differentiate themselves from their previous groups. All in all, Luo people maintain their language and culture wherever they are. The same group that left Anuak land to Lafon Hill and then proceeded to Parjwok, eventually settled in Uganda. There was already another Luo group in Uganda who had settled there from Bahr el Ghazal. They migrated from Luo Dimo (Jur Chol) or Luo people from Wau. The Luo people who live in South Sudan are Acholi, Anuak, Collo, Balanda Boor, Luo Dimo (Jurchol) Maban, Manager, Pari and Shatt (Thur), according to Evans-Pritchard. As stated earlier, Luo people are one tribe, yet they are living in three regions of South Sudan. The Luo people in the Upper Nile region are Anuak, Collo and Maban. Meanwhile Luo groups in Bahr el Ghazal include Balanda Boor, Luo Dimo, Manager and Shatt. Lastly, the Luo people in the Equatoria region are Acholi and Pari.

Luo Diaspora

The Luo migration from the earliest time until the seventeenth century was the main reason for their spread in many countries. As a result, the following countries have Luo citizens:

South Sudan: Acholi, Anuak, Balanda Boor, Luo Dimo, Collo, Maban, Manager, Pari and Shatt.
Uganda: Acholi, Aluro, Lango, Japodoala, and Kunam.
Kenya: Jo-Luo
Democratic Republic of Congo (DRC): Aluro
Ethiopia: Anuak
Egypt: Anu
Tanzania: Jo-Luo

Note: research continues to add more Luos on the list!

2

The Origin Of Anuak Kingdom: Nyic

A foundation of the Anuak monarch began after the capture of Okiro (Ochudho) from a river where boys were fishing. This myth of bringing Ochudho out of water to live in human society was the beginning of the Anuak kingdom. Evans-Pritchard (1940) wrote that "Ochudho came out of the river where boys were disputing about whom the fish belonged to; One boy seized it by the head and another by the tail." Ochudho ordered the boy, who held the fish by the head, to take his hand off. When he did, the fish escaped and went back to the water. However, after losing the fish, Ochudho told them to continue fishing. Not long after, they caught another fish. This time, Ochudho told the boy, who was holding the tail, to let it go. The boy who held fish by the head caught it firmly through the gills and the fish was unable to go back into the water. This judgement of Ochudho impressed not only the boys but also the village elders who heard the news.

According to Ochalla, Okiro lived in a nearby village, approached the river and saw the two boys quarrelling about the fish's ownership. The dispute was not about who caught the fish, but what part of the fish was held to bring it out of the water safely. He watched and then quietly entered the river without the children's knowledge, appearing to the boys to help them solve their quarrel. First, he asked the boy who held the fish's head to take his hand off the fish. Suddenly, the fish escaped through his hand and went back to the river. He told them to keep fishing! When another fish was caught, Okiro asked the other boy who held the tail to remove his hand from the fish. The boys learned that catching the fish through the gills/head made it difficult for the fish to escape. As Okiro delivered his judgement on fishing technique, the boys watched, acknowledged, and accepted the ruling. As a result, Okiro's technique became the most effective method for holding fish.

Okiro wanted to make sure that the boys understood what he had told them. Learning a new and innovative approach took time and its repetition was vital. For that reason, he wanted the effective method of handling fish to be implemented not only by young boys, but for all fishermen in general. The following day, Okiro returned to the river and hid himself in the long grass on the fishing lake's (Pul-Amae) bank, waiting for the boys to come to fish. As he did before, the boys were unaware of his presence. Okiro watched to see whether the boys were effectively judging the rightful of ownership based on who held the head. Cuai was the chief of the Anuak nation where the boys lived. When he heard about Okiro's actions, he ordered councillors of the Bura to follow the boys and bring home the unknown man. The elders told the boys their plans and so while they fished, they pretended to quarrel with each other as they were instructed to do by the elders who were hiding in the grass waiting for Okiro. When Okiro heard the boys arguing about the ownership of a fish, he appeared again to give judgement and was captured.

In the village, Cuai asked him what was his name and where did he come from? Okiro replied but Cuai nicknamed him Ochudho. Okiro told him that he was living in the river where he was caught. Due to his brilliant judgement, Cuai wanted Ochudho to live with them in the village, but he refused. Cuai insisted that he live with them. During a long interrogation, Ochudho told Cuai that he wanted to go back to his family and cattle, which were left in the river. Eventually, Ochudho/Okiro was forced to live in the village against his will.

In Anuak culture, a guest is always given a room or a hut to sleep in at night. Since Ochudho 's arrival in the village, he refused to eat and drink water in public. His hunger strike became a big concern for Cuai and his assistants in the Bura. Finally, Cuai assigned his daughter, Koori, to take care of him. She gave him water in his private room, which he drank. Koori reported back to her father, who told her to prepare food for Ochudho. She cooked food, then served it to Ochudho, which he ate. This development was great news for Cuai. At night, a room was prepared for Ochudho. Koori was told to share a room with him as a caretaker. An Anuak adage says this: "Do not put a hyena with goats in the same house." At night in their private room, Ochudho developed an intimate relationship with Koori and soon she became pregnant. When he realised the daughter of the chief was pregnant, Ochudho feared the consequences, so he disappeared without a trace, suggesting he had gone back to the river from where he came. The reality was most likely that Ochudho returned to his family in another village he never mentioned.

This account is from Ochalla Ojulu Ojwato and has been dismissed by Anuak royal historians. According to the Anuak oral history, Ochudho was the son of river's god. Since the Anuak and Collo kingdoms originated from one source before their settlement in the Upper Nile region, they both believed that when the king dies, he returns to the river. This Luo tradition means that there is another life after death. Onyala (2019) writes: "It is said that Nyikang is the first of the four kings who did not experience death. He simply disappeared into the river and was replaced by his timid elder son, Cal," Onyala said.

Cuai (Founder of Anuak Political Systems)

While Koori was pregnant with Gillo, Ochudho returned to the river and he was not seen again. Nine months later, she delivered a baby boy called Gillo who became the first Anuak king (Evans-Pritchard, 1940). Amae became a lake of blessing that provided fish and had given birth to Ochudho! As written above, it is not only the Anuak kingdom that traces its origins to the river (Nam), but also the Collo kingdom. The Anuak people believed that kingship came directly from god (Jwok Nam) meaning their kingdom came from the

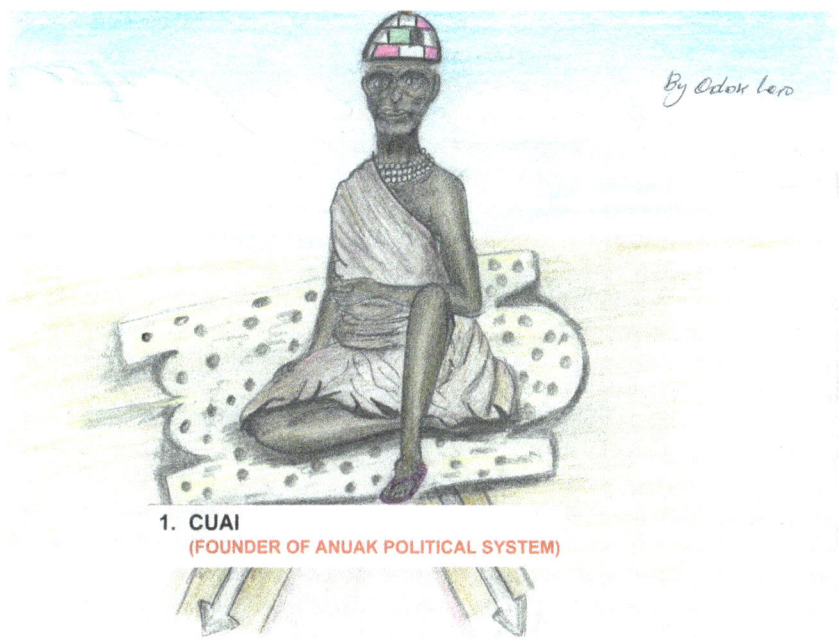

1. CUAI
(FOUNDER OF ANUAK POLITICAL SYSTEM)

god of the river. So, when an Anuak king dies, he is believed to have returned to the river, signifying life after death in Anuak tradition.

Anuak historians knew where Okiro was caught including clan' members who brought him to the village. "Ochudho was caught in Amae. He was captured by certain people in the Anuak community: Jo-Watmaalo Clan (Pokumo), Jo-Watcuai Clan, Jo-Watkanyo Clan came late, yet they were excited about the capture of Ochudho," Akway Agada said. It was believed that Ochudho had no human father, but his father was the god in the river where he was captured and that Ochudho was sent to Anuak society to build the kingdom and install laws and orders for human existence. For that reason, he was commonly referred to as Ochudho-War-Jwok Nam (son of god of the river). It suggested that Ochudho was the god and spirit.

Up to now, it is imperative to understand that every political system is a human invention. However, the Anuak kingdom has linked its existence to god. This belief is held strongly among Anuak, Collo and ancient Egyptians. The system was designed to resolve political issues arising in Anuak society.

Hence, whether its origin is a myth or reality is not relevant. After all, the capture of Ochudho brought an idea that developed the monarchy in the Anuak nation. It was a well-structured political system in Southern Sudan, which defeated the British and kept it free from British colonialism in Africa (Evans-Pritchard,1940). The British defeat is discussed in Chapter 5.

One of the fundamental changes in the political system brought by Ochudho was the formation of rules and laws that lasted for centuries. These rules included prohibiting adultery. Ochudho stated: "It will be a bad thing for a man to take another man's wife. If a man finds another man with his wife, he shall spear him." As the kingdom developed in the following centuries, it adopted policies that dealt with compensation for loss of life and injury. Since the earliest times, when Cuai founded the political system, he made sure that any person who lived in the society was treated equally regardless of his/her background. He also introduced equal treatment for prisoners of war and their protection in the Anuak nation. Moreover, Gurtong was the idea of making peace between the family of victim and offender. It has been the most effective approach to stop retaliation by encouraging compensation for injury or loss of life. The law requires an injured person or families of the deceased to be compensated as a penalty for the crimes committed.

The First Dynasty

The First Dynasty reigned from the fifteenth century to the 1800s. Below are the names of the kings who ruled the Anuak nation until 1855, according to Evans-Pritchard. Ochudho was the founder of the Anuak kingdom but he never ruled. Thus, Gillo his son, was the first king.

1: Gillo Ochudho
2: Opiew
3: Obok
4: Openo
5: Gillo Wara-Akanga
6: Eno
7: Adhiedhi

UNSUNG GIANTS

2. GILLO OCHUDHO
(FOUNDER OF ANUAK KINGDOM)

8: Odol
9. Nyayuak (Female or Queen)
10: Gugo
11: Cham
12: Odola
13: Wango
14: Gillo-Winy-Nyjaango
15: Ajack
16: Gora
(Evans-Pritchard, 1940, p. 82).

The Second Dynasty (1855-1920)

While there is a record of assassinations in the first dynasty, it was more common during the second dynasty. Competition for kingship among royal families turned bloody and they split. Each prince wanted to be a king. This kingship struggle started with Gora's children: Apir, Odiel and Olueth who all aspired to be king and the violent outcome split the family. It is important to acknowledge that during this period, king-slaying for the royal emblems—Ocuok—was common practice. Eventually, Gora's children divided themselves into two royal clans with their lineage traced back to the sons of Gora.

All Anuak's kings traced their roots up to King Gora as their descendant (Evans- Pritchard, 1940). Following their division, Apir Gora founded Tung Nyudola, a royal clan named after Odola, his mother, Akuri's, father. Evans-Pritchard (p. 83) stated that Olueth, identified with the Tung Nyudola lineage because his mother, Amolo, was sister to Akuri. Both sisters were married to King Gora. During their separation, Apir and Olueth went to live with their maternal uncles, people from the Jowat Naadhhi Clan (Evans-Pritchard, 1940, p. 83). The name Tung Nyudola meant descendants of Odola's daughters. Meanwhile, Odiel Gora founded Tung Goch, another royal clan (Evans-Pritchard, p. 83). It was also named after his mother Akwer's father, Goch. When Odiel fought his stepbrothers for kingship, he stayed with his uncles from Jowat Maaaro Clan.

In an interview with Anuak's current king, His Majesty Akway Agada Akway, on 6 June 2019, he described how the kingdom turned bloody marking the start of Agem (a revolution).

According to King Akway, when King Gora passed away, he appointed Apir his heir. Olueth was the second in line to the royal throne. As soon as Apir Gora became king, he was murdered by his half-brother, Odiel Gora. Three of Gora's five sons were not given royal duties by their father, Akway said. However, their exclusion from kingship was a core issue that brought killing and division of the royal family and the split into two clans. He explained that before Gora's death, he wanted his two children—Apir and Olueth—to inherit the throne in the following order:

1: Apir to be the next king.
2: Olueth to be crowned after Apir.
3: Odiel no royal assignment.
4: Athamba no royal assignment.
5: Apar-Nyang no royal assignment.

Odiel violated the royal order of the kingdom. Appointing two successors was meant to reduce the competition of who should be the next king. However, there was a limited chance for a prince to become the king, so some of the princes ignored the previous king's wishes. Odiel assassinated his half-brother, Apir Gora, to become a king marking a period of violent succession. In the next decades, Odiel's revolutionary ideology was practised by many princes. Every prince used violence against the sitting king so that an aspiring candidate could take the throne. "Odiel-winy-Goch killed his brother Apir. After Apir's death, Agango, the son of Apir took power and pursued Odiel and captured him. Due to the crime Odiel had committed, he was sentenced to death. According to him, Agango captured Odiel but later he was killed. However, Gillo-Winy-Metho, the son of Agango cried, begging his own father not to kill Odiel, despite murdering the king. As Gillo cried loudest, 'Odiel asked, why was the boy crying?', Odiel's question was answered in the following statement: 'Gillo-winy-Metho did not want his father to kill you.' Immediately, Odiel called Gillo and spit saliva on his head as a sign of his blessing because Gillo wanted to save his life," Akway explained.

When Gillo-Winy-Metho grew up, he did what Odiel did earlier —he killed his own father and seized power, according to Akway. He asserted: "Later, Gillo-winy-Metho killed his father, Agango, and became the king," he said. King Gillo died of natural causes and he fathered Guro-Obok, Cham-Winyijuu, Gillo-Winy-Waalo, Akane and Nyijango.

In summary, in the First Dynasty, assassination of kings happened less frequently than the Second Dynasty which was marked by dynastic unrest. A deeper analysis of kings slaying one another for the royal emblems indicated that Odiel Gora started a revolution (Agem) against the establishment in the Anuak kingdom when he assassinated his brother. As a result, Odiel started a new era where kingship was taken by force. Furthermore, his revolutionary ideology inspired many princes that led to the cycle of assassinations for decades. It was this destructive politics that caused instability for nearly a century due to power struggle between Tung Goch and Tung Nyudola, the two royal clans. The revolution, which was started by one prince, created instability in the kingship.

At the beginning of the Second Dynasty, there was no peaceful means of transferring power from one king to another. The traditional way of passing power from father to a son had changed completely. So, competition for kingship increased the number of killings in the royal families. It proved that heirs or successors could be killed by another prince to take over the throne. Struggle for kingship not only occurred between two royal families, but also it happened within each clan. For example, one king may have up to ten sons. Among those children, only one son could be crowned at a time.

Impatience with the long wait and no certainty of becoming king, combined with the fear of losing their rank, which would deprive their children of kingship, led to more rebellion in the nation (Evans-Pritchard,1940). Consequently, this revolution was injected into royal politics which marred the kingdom for almost a century. "Cham-Winyijuu took kingship after his father's death. Aganya, a grandson of Odiel attacked Cham," King Akway said. In the middle of the Second Dynasty, Aganya and Cham were rivals during their reigns. Each king wanted to be the most powerful one in the kingdom. At the same time, each king was a representative of their clan. According to Akway, Cham fought Aganya on several occasions. In the first fight, Aganya lost, but the last battle saw Cham killed. "He speared Cham in the neck and the spear broke one of the Ocuok beads," King Akway said.

During the interview with King Akway Agada reiterated that when Cham Gillo was killed, his son, Akway Cham, was too young to take the throne, so his cousin, Metho-Wara- Apilo, became the king in the Adongo region. King Akway explained that the reason for King Cham to bypass his half-brothers in favour of Metho-War-Apilo was due to trust. He said that Cham-Winyijuu and Metho-Wara-Apilo were related in two ways: First, their mothers were from the same clan. Second, Cham and Metho were first cousins because they were grandchildren of Agango. "Apilo and Gillo were half-brothers and they were children of Agango," Akway said. Cham's plan to bring Metho-Wara-Apilo to the throne, suggested that in return, King Metho Apilo would bring his son, Akway Cham to the leadership again. Certainly, it happened! Akway Cham came to power in the Adongo region after his uncle, king Metho was assassinated by King Olimi Aganya (Evans-Pritchard, 1940).

3

The Impact of Firearms

In an interview with his Majesty King Akway Agada Akway, the author asked him how the Anuaks acquired firearms and what impact it had on the kingdom?

The first time an Anuak leader saw a firearm was in the 1880s. It was an unexpected discovery when King Odiel Kwot went hunting and met with Oromo hunters in the forest where Anuak people hunted elephants, leopards, and buffalo. The forests in the Anuak land were full of big game that attracted Ethiopian hunters from the highlands. The Ethiopian hunters carried rifles. After the Oromos and Anuaks met in the forest, the Oromo people wondered how Anuak people killed big games with spears. Meanwhile, King Odiel and his entourage were curious about what Oromo people did with leopard skins and ivory. In Anuak culture, leopard skins were reserved for the kings and chiefs!

Odiel, as king in Abobo at that time, kept leopard skins and ivory in his palace but he took only one leopard skin with him to the hunting camp. He told the Ethiopians that he had many more leopard skins and ivory at home.

To his surprise, the Ethiopians offered Odiel a gun in exchange for the leopard skin he was sitting on, which is how he acquired a firearm.

This accidental meeting between Oromos and the Anuak people brought them closer to each other. While the Oromo people lived on the top of the mountain, the Anuaks lived at the bottom of it but neither nation had never encountered the other before. After Odiel met with the Ethiopians in the hunting camp, he was taken to Gore in Ethiopia by his Oromo friends to show him where they lived. As a courtesy, when it was time for him to come home, Odiel brought some Oromo people to Abobo.

The acquisition of firearms from Ethiopia forged a relationship between the Anuak and Oromo. When the firearm business grew between the two nations, they started to allow for free, peaceful movement between the peoples. Oromo who had Anuak friends were able to come to Pannywaa with their guns and they would go hunting together. Anuaks killed leopards, buffalo or elephants for them, and Oromo gave guns to their friends afterwards. "After a buffalo was killed, they skinned it carefully and took the head of the buffalo to their home in Oromia," Ochalla Ojulu said. It is thought that the Oromo man wanted to show his family and friends at home that he was the hero! "The Oromo people have a tradition of embracing someone who kills a buffalo because he is considered a brave man," Ochalla added. These relations opened more opportunities for the Anuak people to engage in other business with the Ethiopian people for nearly a century between 1880 and 1960.

The Oromo came to Anuak areas to hunt elephants and buffalo and in return brought guns and ammunition to the Anuak people. Oromo people were not familiar with the geographical locations where Anuak people hunted big game. For centuries, the Anuak hunted big game using spears, traps, arrows and bows. "Before obtaining guns, Anuak people trapped leopards with ropes while killing elephants with spears," Ochalla explained. The Oromo trained the Anuak how to use guns and shoot at the targets properly. As the Anuak became more familiar with firearms, they became expert at shooting big game. Eventually, Oromo people started to give their guns to the Anuak men to kill buffaloes and elephants for them. Oromos acknowledged that Anuak marksmen never missed, so they let Anuaks shoot buffalo rather than them wasting their bullets.

Anuaks and the Firearms Business

Business was flourishing between the neighbouring communities. Oromo people would bring extra guns to give any Anuak who could shoot games for them. During the height of guns business, some hunting camps were built where Oromo and Anuak met to trade firearms. In the following years, Anuak people would go to Gore town to sell ivory, leopard skins and honey. In Gore, Anuaks bought clothes, salt, sugar, and Oromo tobacco to take back home. At this moment in time, the Anuak needed more guns to defend their land from Nuer invasion. Meanwhile, the Oromo people needed more ivory, leopard skins and buffalo for economic purposes.

Abobo is one of the villages in the Lul region, close to the Ethiopian border. Odiel Kwot was the crowned king who lived in Abobo in the late eighteenth century. As king, he was an ambitious, intelligent, and patriotic leader. He wanted to push the Nuer people out of the Anuak territory which they had occupied. His plan was to protect the nation from foreign aggression. It was during his reign that Odiel discovered Oromo. Immediately, both communities built peaceful relationships. In honouring their friendship and good brotherhood, Anuak and Oromo named their children after one another.

"Both Anuak and Oromo friends named their children after one another," Ochalla said. This was the reason some Anuaks had Ethiopian names such as Girma, Obole, Abebe, and so on. Likewise, Oromo named their children Omot, Cham, Abella, Abang, respectively. According to Ochalla, throughout that period, each tribe kept those names in their communities.

The first Anuak group to meet Oromo people called them, **Gala**. In Chapter 1, it was mentioned that 90 per cent of Luo names had meaning. In subsequent years, Gala became a common name given by Anuaks to all Ethiopians. Between 1880 and the 1960s, Anuak people worked in Ethiopian coffee plantations and saved money to pay for bride wealth when they returned home. Some of those men named their children Ogala/Agala. Ogala is a male name while Agala is a female name. Naming a child Ogala/Agala indicated that the source of the bride wealth was Oromia. It does not mean there was marriage between Anuaks and Oromo. But it was a symbolic gesture for those who spent years in Ethiopia working hard. It was a recognition for Oromo's hospitality and providing job opportunities that helped some Anuak men to fulfil their marriage requirements back in their country. Equally, Anuaks were selling ivory, leopard skin, gold, and honey to the Ethiopian people. For nearly a century, Anuaks moved back and forth trading with the Ethiopian people in Gore, Bure, and Dembi Dollo. The Oromo people have been a peaceful community and trusted friends to the Anuak people! When trading between Anuak and Oromo nations advanced their mutual interests, it strengthened their relations.

The Anuak people who worked in Ethiopia or traded with the Ethiopian people learned to speak Oromo and Amharic languages. Through diplomatic relations, King Odiel was able to develop a strategic plan to obtain firearms in greater numbers for his armed forces. He decided to equip his Abobo Royal Forces so that they were more advanced in the battlefield than their enemies. After he bought the first collection of guns, Odiel invested heavily in national defence, increasing trade further, so Abobo and its surrounding villages were armed to build a stronger and invincible kingdom. The availability of big game in Anuak's forests enabled the king to purchase more guns and ammunition to arm young men to defend their nation. Firearms from the Oromo people changed the Anuak political system and military capability significantly.

The first two Europeans to visit Anuak country, in 1855, Maltese Andrea Debono and Philippe Terrannvova Antonio found the capital of Anuak kingdom at Umar or Leela in the Adongo region (Evans-Pritchard, 1940, p. 1). For more than 40 years, the Ocuok (royal emblem) was removed from the headquarters and circulated in all five regions—Tiernam, Lul, Baat Gillo, Nyikani, and Adongo. It became a mobile emblem that travelled with kingship from one region to another. In the Second Dynasty, no king held Ocuok longer because other princes wanted emblems for themselves. In the Anuak kingdom, a prince became king only when he held the Ocuok emblems, which gave him legitimacy to govern. Thus, kingship and Ocuok were inseparable. As a rule, there was no parallel reign in the Second Dynasty. Odiel Kwot's reign was the first time a king held royal emblems for years since it was uprooted from Leela after 1855. Odiel Kwot was, from 1897, the most powerful king in the nation, controlling the royal emblems for many years. Although other princes attempted to seize them, they could not manage to face his well-armed men in Abobo. His forces were equipped with modern weapons to fight any group which wanted to take Ocuok away from his village. In this case, nobody attacked Odiel's residency because rivals knew that he had firearms, while potential attackers still relied on spears. As a result, King Odiel remained unchallenged for years until he voluntarily gave Ocuok to his own brother, according to Evan-Pritchard.

After King Odiel introduced firearms in Paanywaa, other leaders followed suit. Olimi Aganya was the second king in the country to obtain firearms. With the aid of firearms, King Olimi was able to maintain royal emblems at Ajwara in the Adongo region, but later he moved to Digira in the Tiernam region. In the Anuak political realm, it was crucial to realise that keeping the royal emblems required power because a village that held Ocuok became the primary target for aspirants to the throne. A thorough examination of the Anuak political system revealed that, in the Second Dynasty, competition for the royal emblems and supremacy of the land was limited to three kings who acquired guns before anyone else (Evans-Pritchard, 1940). Those locations that had guns, while other villages still depended on spears, had the advantage, which meant three kings dominated the political arena.

King Olimi-Wara-Aganya was the second leader who purchased firearms, after he followed Odiel, who brought the first firearms to Anuak land. With availability of guns in his palace, Olimi intimidated members of the Tung Nyudola clan in the Adongo region. According to Evans-Pritchard, King Olimi's cruelty and violence made the Adongo region unsafe for King Metho-Wara-Apilo and his two nephews, Prince Akway Cham and Prince Abella Gillo. Those individuals were forced to flee to Gok in the Lul region seeking refuge in Ethiopia. King Akway said that when they arrived at the Ethiopian border, they decided to send King Metho Apilo back so that Olimi could not claim the people in Adongo as his subjects. While Metho Apilo agreed to return to Ajwara, Akway Cham and Abella Gillo proceeded to Ethiopia. The decision for King Metho to return home was a high-risk strategy because King Olimi was terrorizing everyone in the region, according to Evans-Pritchard.

Despite the risk, King Metho returned. In the middle of the Second Dynasty, he became the only king in Adongo at that time! "Metho-Wara-Apilo decided to sacrifice his life so his blood would bless Akway Cham to be a powerful leader," King Akway said. Before he returned home, however, King Metho and Akway discussed important security issues and how to resolve them. The resolutions of their meeting outlined key issues of security and politics: First, acquisition of firearms. Second, a military response to Olimi's aggression. Third, they wanted to maintain grassroot support in the Adongo region. To implement these plans, King Metho knew that if something happened to him on his return, his nephew, Akway Cham, would take the throne and restore the dignity of their royal family. Unfortunately, not too long after Metho returned to Adongo, he was assassinated by King Olimi Aganya in an ambush between Akwaralak and Nyium (Evans-Pritchard,1940, p. 92).

According to King Akway Agada, King Olimi Aganya vowed to kill anyone from Tung Nyudola! After the assassination of King Metho, Akway Cham and Abella Gillo were Olimi's next target. Both men fled to Gok and later Akway travelled to Abobo to meet King Odiel Kwot to find out how he could acquire firearms. Akway's mother, Ogatu, was related to King Odiel. King Akway Agada revealed that both Ogatu and Odiel were from the Tung Goch lineage. So, Akway Cham and King Odiel Kwot were nephew and uncle. Odiel warmly welcomed Akway and in their private talks, Akway explained what had happened to him. He wanted to acquire firearms for self-defence! "Odiel said to Akway Cham, Oromo people wanted buffalo, ivory and leopard skins," King Akway Agada stated. He asserted that "Oromos came to Anuak villages near the Ethiopian border with guns and ammunition and gave guns to the Anuak people who shot buffalo or elephants for them," he said.

While Akway Cham was in Abobo, "he found a dead elephant in the forest. The tusks from a dead elephant were worth 25 guns and ammunition," he said. This is what he had been looking for and mission accomplished! Now, Akway used one of the 25 guns to hunt more buffalo, elephants, and leopards. In less than a month, he shot his first elephant and sold its ivory for another 25 guns. Great opportunities began opening for Akway Cham that enabled him to buy more guns. While he was hunting in Gok forests, Akway heard that King Olimi had sent his delegation to Ethiopia carrying ivory and leopard skins for him. King Akway asserted that, "Olimi sent his people to Ethiopia carrying ivory. Akway Cham ambushed them and seized ivory from them." During his time in Lul region, Akway Cham bought 800 guns when he was in Gok according to his grandson, the current king Akway Agada Akway.

Anuak Diplomacy

As King Odiel discovered Ethiopian hunters in the forest and travelled to Gore town with them, he built a mutual relationship with the Ethiopian authority there. He used to go to Gore directly to buy things that he needed. In those days, Odiel was the only Anuak leader known to the Ethiopian people. But after Olimi managed to follow in his footsteps and purchased firearms too, Odiel's relation with the Ethiopian government in Gore turned sour. Evans-Pritchard (1940) reported that, in 1906, King Odiel was arrested and detained in Gore. The Ethiopian government had transferred its allegiance to King Olimi Aganya. For the reasons known to the Ethiopian people, they supported Olimi instead of Odiel, the person they had known for 26 years. It could have been a competition over kingship and power struggles in the Anuak kingdom.

Power struggles among Anuak leaders led to betrayal of one another in Gore town. King Akway Agada states that when Akway Cham bought guns from an Oromo gun dealer in the black market, Olimi was angry. Olimi considered that an enemy was arming himself for potential war who could have been a real threat to his reign. To stop Akway's plan, Olimi influenced the Gore authority to impose higher taxation on him. But Akway Cham refused to pay high taxes; instead, he would pay like everyone else. According to King Akway Agada, Olimi feared that Akway Cham might be preparing to attack him.

The two men could clearly not trust each other. First, Olimi chased out Akway Cham from Obuothi and Kintha in Tiernam up to Otalo in the Adongo region. For his personal security, he took refuge at Gok village in Lul region (Evans-Pritchard, 1940). When he came to Abobo for firearms, Akway ambushed Olimi's Supporters and took ivory and leopard skins in retaliation for Olimi's aggression. Olimi convinced the Ethiopian authorities to arrest and detain Akway Cham in Gore. King Odiel heard of nephew's arrest and sent his delegation to Gore to negotiate his release with the Ethiopian authority. It was the most difficult negotiation. The unsuccessful talks made the delegation worry about Akway Cham's fate in Ethiopian detention. As a last resort, the Anuak people successfully bribed Ethiopian officials to release him, King Akway revealed.

After his release from detention, the Ethiopian authority tried to reconcile King Olimi and Prince Akway, but this attempt at peace failed. Not even a friendly gesture such as a handshake was impossible. Prince Akway refused to shake hands with King Olimi, saying that he could not shake hands with the man who killed his uncle. This rejection was seen by the Ethiopian authority as well as King Olimi as a serious threat to Olimi's leadership.

It was Odiel's support that freed Akway Cham from detention in Ethiopia. King Odiel did his best to help him before he was taken to prison. It is worth mentioning that Odiel, himself, had been detained in Gore previously in 1906 (Evans-Pritchard, 1940). From his personal experience, he was able to send the delegation to negotiate for Prince Akway's release. King Odiel was a true uncle and concerned leader who cared about his people even in another country.

4

Firearms Change Everything

The introduction of firearms into Anuak nation revolutionized their political systems. It is crucial to understand that while monarchy existed for centuries, there was no central government in the Anuak system. There was the king but no unified kingdom. In other words, the central government to bring all Anuaks under one ruler was in progress (Evans-Pritchard, 1940). Every state was independent politically and led by a governor. The first Anuak leaders who obtained guns from Ethiopia were able to defend themselves more effectively against the Nuers. They carried out counterattacks into the Nuerland (Evans-Pritchard, 1940). The kings in the Second Dynasty were determined to remove Nuer people from the Anuak land they occupied and stop Nuer territorial expansion by pushing them back to their original homes at Bul Nuer in Bentiu. "The introduction of firearms led to the amalgamation of small local groups, in the villages and some districts. Nobles who managed to acquire firearms were able to establish effective control over other villages than their own," said Evans-Pritchard. He said these political changes enabled the Anuak people to utilize their new weapons effectively against the Nuer and

Murle who raided their villages. The leaders who came to the political arena in the 1900s strengthened their unity and focused on external aggression. They adopted new policies that appeared more effective in resolving land issues with the Nuers.

Nuers' Invasion of Nyium Region (Nasir)

When Anuak people moved from Malakal, they started their settlements from Gillo Aciel, Abwong, Ulang, Beet and Jang-Mer. Anuaks built from the Nyium region to Okwa and Okwach in the Ternam region. They also built from Nyium to Gambella and Bonga in Openo state. According to Collins, in the eighteen century, Baqqara Arabs arrived in Southern Sudan from Chad to settle in the north and west of Nuer and Dinka who lived along the Bahr El Ghazal and Bahr Al-Arab. Not too long after their settlement in the area, Baqqara Arabs began raiding for cattle and slaves among the Nuer and Dinka (Collins, 1983). In 1850, a larger population of Bul Nuer moved to the east. This migration pushed Jikany Nuer and eventually they reached Nyium state in Anuak land. The Nuer invasion was a major concern, which Anuak leaders needed to resolve diplomatically or militarily.

In 1880, King Odiel Kwot armed his forces with guns that replaced traditional weapons such as spears. He planned to stop Nuer territorial expansion into Anuak country as Anuak political leaders realized that there was an urgent need to confront the Nuer people militarily. They vowed to kick them out of Nyium state. By this time, some Anuaks who lived in Nyium were leaving their ancestral land because of the Nuer occupation. But most of them remained in Nyium and Anuaks are currently still living with the Nuers. This was a critical issue that required national co-operation from every Anuak leader in the country.

Evans-Pritchard (1940) studied kingship and headmanship in the Anuak society. He found that Anuaks had a well-structured political system in kingship and headmanship. When he compared Anuak political systems with Nuer politics, he found the opposite. He states that Nuer people lived in an acephalous society where there was no concept of state, kingship, or any form of political organization. Evans-Pritchard wrote: "In a Nuer village, or in any other local Nuer group, there is no head of the community. No one personifies the collective interests and loyalties of the group." In Anuak, loyalties are built in the political system that protect the collective interests of every citizen in the country (Evans-Pritchard, 1940, p. 136). But without a system in place, there was no loyalty or allegiance. There was no way to build loyalty in this acephalous world of pastoralism and nomadic. Anarchy exists among nations without states. Overall, the Nuers never developed political organization to govern themselves properly (Evans-Pritchard,1940). "The Nuer system is acephalous, and this is evidence in its smallest, no less than in its larger, political groups," he writes.

Since 1850, Nuer and Anuak had been at war because of this territorial expansion. Anuak people have the biggest land that stretches from Adongo in the south all the way to Lul/Thim region in the East. In the northern part of the country, the Openo region borders Ethiopia on the side of Dembi Dollo and Bure. Therefore, all villages such as Ulang, Beet, Jang-Mer and so forth were homes of the Anuak people for centuries before Nuers invasion in 1850 (Collins, 1983). As previously discussed, Anuaks had eleven regions/states in their federation: Adongo, Baat Gillo, Ciro, Lul/Thim, Jor, Nyikani, Nyium, Ojwa, Openo, Rwanye, and Tiernam. Each region was led by different leaders who played an important role in politics and national security. The Anuak political system varied from one region to another or even within the same region. But many of the regions were led by headmen (chiefs) while kingship dominated Adongo and Tiernam regions with exceptions of Abobo in Lul state and Elngo in Baat Gillo region respectively (Evans-Pritchard, 1940).

Liberating Nyium State from Occupation

King Odiel Kwot led the liberation of Nyium to disperse Nuer people from Anuak land. He was the first king to use rifles on the battlefield. The acquisition of firearms had resulted in political changes that had built a nationalist mindset. King Odiel led his forces against the Nuers who had settled in the west of Anuak land, attacking Jikany Nuer (Evans-Pritchard, 1940). His foreign expedition encouraged every leader to focus on pushing the Nuer people back to their own land. As Odiel's forces used advanced weapons, the Anuak people were in a better position to inflict heavy losses on the Nuer people. After Odiel returned home, another king attacked the same Nuer group. All Anuak leaders, regardless of their locations, had the ultimate goal to push Nuers out of their land.

When King Olimi Aganya obtained firearms, he also attacked Gaajak Nuer, but he was killed during the fight (Evans-Pritchard, 1940, p. 11). King Odiel and king Olimi both fought against the Jikany Nuer, but there was no outright success, according to Evans-Pritchard, despite a heavy toll on the Nuers. However, this was a reminder that the Anuak people would continue to attack Nuer people until they left their land.

Democracy in The Anuak lands

Every Anuak village was independence, which shows a genuine democratic freedom in Anuak society. However, more political freedom created weakness to the overall security of the Anuak nation. Before acquiring firearms, the Anuak people lived in their independent villages and no powerful leaders controlled neighbouring villages (Evans-Pritchard, 1940). This political isolation had weakened national defence as there was no co-operation among them. Each region was an independent state and had no connection with other regions. Henceforth, the weakness of the central government to oversee and monitor security was a real concern in the Second Dynasty.

Gradually, three prominent kings who brought guns to the country dedicated themselves to improve the security situation once and for all. They learnt that to defend their country better, they needed to restructure their security system to protect all citizens. This meant breaking down independent villages to build stronger unity, which saw the creation of the formidable army known as Adongolese Royal Army (Evans-Pritchard, 1940). This moving away from traditional village freedom indicated that King Akway Cham was preparing to build a modern army that protected Anuak people in their country. Evans-Pritchard noted: "Living in independent village communities, frequently fighting each other, the Anuak were unable to combine a large enough scale of forces or for long enough to resist aggression and have consequently been subjected to frequent invasions and raids from their neighbours."

Building the strong army for interdependent villages was the policy of King Akway Cham when he came to power. He was the chief architect of breaking down leadership structures of the smaller villages to build stronger administration in the Adongo region. As a result, he introduced inter-village relations that allowed all Adongolese people to come together for self-defence (Evans-Pritchard, 1940). The new policy worked by cultivating unity and loyalty to the entire Adongo region instead of just within one village. King Akway established a nation capital in Otalo, and he provided guns to people who lived far from the capital. This enhanced not just loyalty to him, but also to the Adongo region at large. As regional loyalty grew, the next step was to embrace nationalism. Eventually, his new policy broke down individual's loyalty to their own villages and the Adongolese people pledged their allegiance to the Adongo region and Anuak nation as whole. The goal was to protect all Anuaks irrespective of the region they reside in.

Decentralisation in The Anuak Kingdom

The Anuak political system is more decentralized with no central government. Evans-Pritchard (1940) stated that most of the villages were politically independent and economically self-contained, suggesting that Anuak people developed a statehood that was self-reliant. They structured a political system that could exist independently without support from outside.

There are two political systems that govern the Anuak nation- Kwar (headmanship/chiefdom) which rules most parts of the country, while kingship (Nyic) dominates the eastern part, particularly the Adongo and Tiernam states. Details about the Kwar political system will be discussed in Chapter 10. "In this part of the country we may speak of an inter-village organization with the emblems as its integrative element. The villages are politically independent, but they are not like in the west, politically isolated," Evans-Pritchard wrote. The royal emblems have important value in Anuak culture because they are linked to the coronation and prestige of the kings. Those royal emblems include five string of beads, four spears, two stools, drum, and the Ocuok, the most important of all the necklaces (Evans-Prichard,1940). Even though each material has its own function, they are inseparable. "They cannot be distributed among a number of nobles. The kingship is indivisible. This allowed only one king at a time who was the holder of all the emblems. They can circulate but there cannot be more than one king at the same time," Evans- Pritchard writes.

The Anuak federation strongly supported independence of each region with an independent administrative unit under a particular chief or king. Note that when a king loses ownership of the royal emblems, he maintains his title. He is still the legitimate king where he lives. But the decentralized system limits the capacity of powerful leaders to control other neighbouring regions. In addition, the political system gives rights to the leadership of the clan—the ruling family—in their land. Anuak's division of power makes the federal government weaker, while empowering local governments. It restricts one leader becoming more powerful than other leaders in the country. This notion prevents leaders from abusing their power. Similarly, some studies in political science suggest that when two different leaders have equal power, they are inclined to respect each other. It is obvious that unlimited power under dictatorships can be disastrous.

Firearms Disrupting Political Balance

As mentioned earlier, the acquisition of rifles radically changed Anuak political systems. The first Ocuok holders when firearms were introduced are listed below. It was the second circulation of the royal emblems among the kings throughout the nation. King Odiel Kwot who lived in Abobo was the first person to obtain rifles from Ethiopia. In 1897, he was the most powerful king in the nation and highly respected (Evans-Prichard, 1940, p. 11). King Olimi Aganya was the second king to acquire guns. Each king attacked Nuers at different times. But they did not coordinate their attacks against the Nuer people. King Akway Cham was the last king to obtain firearms, yet he was the most successful king in his military expeditions (Evans-Pritchard, 1940, p.11).

In the Second Dynasty, transferring royal emblems from the incumbent king to a new king can be peaceful or violent. The following is the order of the emblem's movement from one king to another:

1: Odiel Kwot kept Ocuok with him in Abobo, Ethiopia.
2: He gave Ocuok to his half-brother, also called Odiel Kwot.
3: Odiel passed them over to another brother named Kwot.
4: Akway Akway Gang captured them during a raid of Kwot's village. For years, royal emblems rotated among the brothers only. In the end, Akway, a king from Tung Nyudola lineage, who resided in Gok, Ethiopia, seized Ocuok from Kwot, according to Evans-Pritchard.
5: Akway passed them on to a member of his clan. Oduru-War-Obaang-Winyidoor, kept emblems with him at Pinythin in South Sudan.
6: Nyang (Gora) Aganya took them from Oduru and passed them on to Olimi Aganya in Ajwara in South Sudan, but later Olimi moved to Digira in Ethiopia.
7: King Akway Cham attacked King Olimi at Digira and seized Ocuok from him in 1910 (Evans-Pritchard, 1940). After he attacked Digira and destroyed Olimi's palace, surprisingly, the royal emblems were not there. Those royal emblems were kept somewhere in Otalo where Akway Cham resided. It was discovered that a friend of Olimi kept the royal emblems with him in Otalo. "Ocuok was hidden in Nyigwo Goro Chweere's house in Otalo," King Akway Agada said. Akway-War- Cham took Ocuok from Olimi's friend and he kept them in Otalo in South Sudan. This marked the total defeat of King Olimi Aganya who was the most influential leader in the Tiernam region. It was the end of enmity and intimidation of the Adongolese people. After a long struggle for freedom, King Akway proved that he was an invincible king who radically changed Anuak history forever. His victory over King Olimi was his first, but he went on to achieve more victories during his reign.

King Odiel Attacked King Akway Cham in Otalo

The arrival of firearms broke down the chain of command that Olimi and Odiel had previously enjoyed. Unbalanced power in the political game showed that King Akway Cham now led the Second Dynasty. But he had to prove whether he could maintain supremacy. After he took the royal emblems successfully from King Olimi, the battle was not over. For years, King Akway Cham and King Olimi Aganya were political rivals. Each leader wanted to defeat the other. Losing political power to King Akway Cham was a serious threat to all kings of the Tung Goch Clan. As King Olimi lost royal emblems to Akway-war-Cham, he also lost supremacy of the land.

Three months after Akway seized the royal emblems from King Olimi at Dirgia in Tiernam region, his official coronation took place in Otalo. His ambition to become a king made him endure many trials and tribulations. As the holder of the emblems, he would face many more challenges in days, months, and years to come. An immediate challenge to his kingship was a military alliance formed to defeat him so the royal emblems would go to the Tung Goch Clan, according to Evans-Pritchard. While Olimi lost Ocuok to King Akway, he was later killed in the battle with the Nuers leaving the Tiernam state without a powerful leader. However, King Odiel at Abobo in Lul region, from the same clan with late king Olimi, combined forces to attack Otalo. In the absence of Olimi, King Odiel led the coalition forces (Evans-Pritchard, 1940). Before the attack, Odiel campaigned for military action against King Akway Cham and King Gora Aganya, a brother of Olimi, responded by sending his forces to support Odiel. But Gora himself did not fight due to his sickness, according to Evans-Pritchard. In addition, Anyoonya Odiel joined Tung Goch's alliance (Evans-Pritchard,1940). Now three kings from Tung Goch combined their forces to attack Otalo.

Meanwhile, members of the Tung Nyudola Clan organized their forces to support King Akway Cham. This military confrontation was built on traditional rivalries of Tung Nyudola Vs. Tung Goch. For that reason, King Obaang-war-Winyidoor sent his forces with his son, Oduru, to fight alongside King Akway's forces (Evans-Pritchard,1940). At the same time, Abella Gillo also joined the military alliance of Tung Nyudola forces. It was the first time in Anuak politics that leaders joined forces with their royal clans.

The battle to take the royal emblems from Akway Cham proved difficult. Rumours of an attack reached Otalo before the enemies came and Akway was prepared for the war. "When Akway heard that Odiel was advancing, he went out of Otalo to Ajwara to meet him. Meanwhile, Odiel approached along the course of the Oboth river passing Ajwara and attacked the undefended village of Otalo, burning a greater part of it to the ground. King Akway returned in haste to Otalo and shooting went on all morning. At midday Odiel's men went down to the Oboth to drink water and fighting resumed in the afternoon and continued till dusk. The next morning the attacking forces departed," said Evans-Pritchard.

The fighting lasted for two days! Finally, Tung Goch's forces were defeated (Evans-Pritchard, 1940, p. 94). King Akway Cham was able to keep the royal emblems in Otalo until his death. His victory did not come easily. It was a disciplined determination to free Adongolese people from King Olimi Aganya's intimidations and threats. Defeating the two most powerful kings from Tung Goch demonstrated that King Akway was the most powerful king in the country. As a champion, he was recognized as the king of kings in the kingdom and became the leader of all kings by the end of the Second Dynasty. Political change had ended bloodshed between rival villages and stopped assassinations of the crowned king because King Akway Cham became more powerful than his political rivals. Every prince who wished to be crowned would come to Otalo for their coronation.

Renewed Focus on The Nuer invasion

King Akway Cham built the national army to protect Anuak land from every corner!

In 1911, following his coronation, Akway led Adongolese forces to Nuer Lou and Jikany Nuer in a well-organized attack that devastated the enemies (Evans-Pritchard, p, 11). His military action was the most effective at clearing out Nuer people from the land they occupied, according to Evans-Pritchard. He wrote: "Akway's foreign expeditions were uniformly successful." At the end of the year, Akway's forces chased Nuer people all the way to Al-Zaraf (Fangak) and he returned to Akobo with hundreds of Nuer captives and thousands of cattle (Evans-Pritchard, p. 11). Furthermore, Akway and his forces went deeper inside the Nuer territory and attacked their villages. For the first time since the Nuer invasion, Nuer people encountered the deadliest attack they had ever seen. After King Akway returned from Nuerland, Anuak people from the Ciro region carried out another extensive raid to push Nuers away from their land. "Another raid was carried out by the Anuaks of Ciro district against Lou Nuer and attacks on the Jikany Nuer," Evans-Pritchard reported.

During the reign of King Akway Cham, Nuer territorial expansion into Anuak land was being halted successfully, however, the plan was disrupted and stopped by the British. If the British had not interfered in the Anuak-Nuer territorial wars, the Nuer would have been pushed back to their own lands. Anuaks tried all diplomatic means to resolve issues peacefully, none of the approaches worked with Nuers. Various agreements were signed between the two nations, but every one of them was violated. It showed that failed agreements with the Nuer people were rooted in their acephalous nation where there was no Nuer leader in charge. The acephalous society of Nuer was a breeding ground for anarchy and violence! Since there was nobody responsible for the Nuer nation, Anuak people carried out deadly attacks on them (Evans-Pritchard, 1940). The colonial government in Sudan intervened to protect Nuers. The Nuer people were British subjects who paid taxes to the colonial government. Yet, they endured injustice and brutality in colonial rule. As the British taxpayers, their masters had no choice but to go after King Akway in Otalo. The British pursued King Akway Cham with the intention of disarming him and bringing Nuer captives or prisoners of war back to the Nuerland (Evans-Pritchard, 1940).

5

British Defeated in The Battle of Juom

The British colonial forces attacked the Anuak kingdom in 1912. Their intention was to punish King Akway Cham for attacking Nuer invaders in Anuak land. The British planned travel to Otalo to capture King Akway Cham and bring him to the British authority in chains! Before the British departure, the Anuak people in Akobo warned King Akway Cham of the British plan to attack Otalo in Adongo's headquarters. Based on the report, King Akway declared Dhaldiim, which means resistance to colonization. **Dhaldiim** is a compound word: **Dhal** meaning resistance; **Diim** meaning colonization or injustice.

The Anuak kingdom was established four hundred years before the British arrival in Sudan! It developed policies and regulations that governed the Anuak nation for centuries. According to King Akway Cham, British colonization which aimed to impose its own rules on the Anuak people was unacceptable. The Anuaks believed that their kingdom was equal to any kingdom in Europe. According to Diop, kingship and religious ideology started in Egypt but later adapted by white people. Diop (1989) proved that Ancient Egyptians were the source of civilization due to their technical development, scientific and military power. So, they became a powerful nation in the world. However, Blacks' power declined over the centuries. "The Black race, long the numerous, first overpowered and dominated Whites; but the latter, having gradually multiplied, shook off the yoke of their masters. The ex-slaves, becoming master in his turn, condemned the Blacks to bear the chains that he had just broken," Diop said.

To defend their kingdom from British colonization, King Akway prepared to resist the British invasion. He planned to meet the British forces outside of Otalo to avoid casualties among women, children and the elderly. It was a well-prepared mission embarked on with bravery and commitment to remain free from foreign control. The British expedition against the Anuak nation proved to be the deadliest war ever the British faced, not only in Sudan but anywhere in the African continent.

The Battle at Juom

In 1912, the British troops were dispatched to attack King Akway Cham in Otalo, according to Evans-Pritchard. Meanwhile Adongolese royal forces prepared to meet the British forces at Juom. On the battlefield, the British forces suffered heavy losses including the killing of two leading officers who commanded their forces (Evans-Pritchard,1940). Even though the exact number of British troops killed in the Battle of Juom was not released, Anuaks remembered British who were killed in the Juom attack, King Akway said. Anuaks counted the number of guns, different to the Anuak firearms, that were captured from the British after the war was over. Some guns might be dropped by wounded soldiers, but it was reasonable to estimate how many British were killed in the Juom offensive—"100 British soldiers were killed. This figure was known because more than a hundred guns were captured during the fight," King Akway Agada stated. In Anuak culture, war is the last resort after peaceful means failed. They knew that war always brought casualties on both sides, regardless of who won or lost the war. According to King Akway, the Anuak people admitted that many of them were killed by the British, a number almost equal to the British casualties.

According to the Anuak veterans, the British initially had the upper hand in the war. However, a simple strategy reversed the tragic fate. At the first hour of their fighting, Anuaks realized that British troops were riding on horses! So, they ran very fast. The speed of the horses helped them to run easily and changed their positions quickly. The Anuak marksmen or snipers had a hard time shooting at their target precisely. "After the war became bloody, King Akway Cham ordered his armed men to shoot horses first. This strategy worked better," King Akway Agada said. The new strategy was to kill their horses first so that British troops would be on the ground. Implementing the new military tactics enabled snipers to bring the British to their level and the marksmen used their skills to shoot them. The tactic not only grounded the British soldiers but often disarmed them as well as they fell from their horses. As casualties kept rising among the British troops, they had no other option but to retreat and accept defeat. Consequently, the colonial forces withdrew from the battlefield, annihilated by the Adongolese people (Evans-Pritchard, 1940).

A few months later, after the British defeat at Juom, they tried again to penetrate through the Nyikani region but the leaders of Nyikani combined their forces to face the military might of the British empire. Again, it was another deadly war. After heavy fighting, the British pushed the Anuaks of Nyikani in that fight. Evans-Pritchard (1940) wrote that some villages were burnt down, but the British did not win. "Their villages were burnt, but all efforts to get to the people and their cattle in the swamps proved unavailing," Evans-Pritchard wrote. In this second attempt to invade Anuak land, the British learned that the Anuak people did not want them anywhere in their country. There was no soft landing for the British people anywhere in the Anuak land! As a result, the British were repelled from Nyikani region, and they went back to their base in Akobo in the Ciro region. Finally, the British conceded military defeat in Anuak land! Overall, the Anuak people in Southern Sudan were free from British control (Collins, 1983).

The Tomb of Anuak's King

A king is buried with honour and dignity. The process of burying the king is different from a commoner (Bang). The tomb of the king (Nyiya/Rwoth) is constructed in a special way. A deep hole is dug, and strong poles are laid on the ground to build the foundation. The first platform is built to ensure that the king's corpse never touches the ground (Evans-Pritchard, 1940, p. 71). After the first layer is complete, a bed is built to make enough room between the first and second layers. The next step is to lay the animal's skins on the first bed. A second platform is designed like a bed for the king's corpse. Evans-Pritchard writes: "Skins are laid on the platform as a couch for the corpse which is covered with more skins." A third platform is built to prevent soil from falling on the king's body. This is not the end of the burial construction! A house is built on the top of the tomb. Viewing it from a distance, it looks like a house, but inside is the king's tomb.

Finally, a fence is built around the house for better protection. But there is a small passage that allows a person to enter the perimeter for cleaning and to regularly smooth out the king's tomb with sand. To maintain cleanliness of the tomb, a custodian is assigned to sweep the burial site (Eavns-Pritchard,1940, p. 71). "The Anuak word for the king's death is gone to the river." This means that kingship came from the river; inferring that the king is going back to the river at the end of his life. Both Anuak and Collo believe that the kingship was sent to human society by the god of the river.

Akway Cham's Legacy

King Akway Cham left the kingdom secure, stable, and flourishing. He made the greatest achievements in the history of the Anuak kingdom than any king who served before him. After his death, it was the first time in the Second Dynasty period for a 12-year-old boy to lead the nation. When Akway was a young man, he was almost killed by King Olimi Aganya. But later he dealt with him successfully (Evans-Pritchard, 1940). He brought the aggressive king to his knees! When King Odiel Kwot became a representative of Tung Goch clan, leading the coalition forces against King Akway Cham in Otalo, King Akway Cham defeated this second powerful king.

King Akway efficiently dealt with internal and external difficulties politically or militarily. His first political mission was to secure the royal emblems that would give him legitimacy to unite the kingdom. Despite a century of parallel reign in the kingdom, King Akway had a strong vision that the Anuak nation should be ruled by one leader at a time, a vision that became more conceivable thanks to the acquisition of firearms. King Akway Cham used his will to dictate who should take over the throne after his death. His will was used to reduce competition among his sons after he died. However, not all the princes agreed with what their father said. Each prince believed that he was a son of the king and he should be a king too.

In his will, he appointed some of his children to inherit the throne in the following order:

1. Cham-Wara-Akello
2. Gillo-War-Orow
3. Agada-War-Dikang
4. Cham-Wara-Achalla, no royal assignment
5. Agole-Winy-Nyubak, no royal assignment

King Akway Cham had 12 sons in total. For example, Cham-wara-Akello means a son of Akello. The word Wara/War is like a title or a courtesy to a king or headman. All kings and headmen are addressed with their mothers' names: King Cham-wara-Akello. While his given name is Cham Akway.

The king died of natural causes in 1920. His successor was Cham Akway, a little boy according to Evans-Pritchard. Losing the bravest king was an opportunity for the British to come to Otalo after 14 years of being blocked by the powerful King Akway Cham. One year after King Akway died, the British arrived in Pochalla in 1921 (Evans-Pritchard, 1940).

"I found the youthful sultan squatting on a heap of leopard skins strewn on a raised mud platform awaiting my arrival. He was attired in a red and gold robe of honour given to his father by the Abyssinians; on his head he wore a headdress surmounted by the long feathers of the secretary bird, feathers which alone are worn by the sultan, and across his face hung rows of cowrie shells," Lt. Colonel. C. R. K. Bacon, a British military administrator, wrote .

As the youngest king, King Cham Akway was more susceptible to attack from older kings. It is worth mentioning that while King Cham-Wara-Akello was in Otalo, his father also crowned Cham Metho to lead in Ajwara. This is what late King Metho Apilo anticipated for his son.

Bacon promised to support the young king in case of attack. "Bacon announced that he had recognition and support of the government, of which he gifted him [King Cham] with regimental sash and sword," wrote Evans-Pritchard. Giving King Cham the medal of honour meant he became the king of kings in the Anuak nation. Additionally, Bacon suggested that the colonial government should support only one king for the whole tribe. Evans-Pritchard asserted that in 1925, "Bacon urged that King Cham Akway be given every encouragement and dignity and that his position be upheld for considerable influence over the tribe as a whole. This could be of great assistance in the formation and organization of native courts."

The Third Dynasty (1921-2021)

King Cham Akway was the youngest person ever to rule the kingdom and his rule marked the start of the Third Dynasty. When the British colonial government established its administration in Pochalla in 1921, they realized that Ethiopian government did not exist in the Baro (Openo) and Akobo borderland (Collins,1983, p. 368-369). It was shocking for the British officials to see that the Ethiopian government could not be found anywhere in the Anuak country. It proved that Anuak people were truly independent. In the early 1900s, Anuaks built diplomatic relations with Oromo people in Gore town by trading ivory and leopard skins. But the Ethiopian government did not penetrate the Anuak country. It was only trade agreements that brought the two nations together.

Due to their mutual interests, an Ethiopian governor at Gore facilitated easy access for the Anuak people to buy guns and ammunition in Ethiopia. It was a win-win deal because Ethiopian authorities-imposed taxation on the Anuak leaders who purchased rifles. Hence, the common interests of Anuak and Oromo brought them closer. After all, the Anuak people who lived near the Ethiopian border were not subjects of Emperor Menelik, nor did the

Ethiopian kingdom rule the Anuak land (Evans-Pritchard, 1940). Despite the clear evidence that Anuak had never been part of Ethiopia, the British colonial administration in Sudan insisted on implementing the agreement that was signed in 1902 between Menelik and Anglo-Egyptian Sudan (Collins, 1983). That agreement divided Anuaks between Ethiopia and Sudan. So, when the colonial government strengthened its presence in Anuak land in Sudan, it also wanted the Ethiopian government to control Anuak people in Gambella in Ethiopia.

In an interview with Ojwok Agada Akway on May 16, 2019, he was asked why the Ocuok (royal emblem) was rotating among Colonial appointed kings, finally taken back to Otalo where it currently sits?

The British gloated over the death of King Akway Cham, a king who defeated them militarily and the colonial government came to Otalo through political deception and manipulation, Ojwok said. They took advantage of the young and inexperienced king Cham-Wara-Akello. Unfortunately, the young King Cham became an easy prey for the British people who were defeated by his father 14 years earlier (Evans-Pritchard, 1940). Ojwok suggested that the colonial administration planned to avenge their defeat at the battle of Juom and sent a delegation to the crowned king in Otalo inviting him to a meeting in Pochalla, Ojwok said. The meeting took place in 1925.

The British deliberately planned to move King Cham far away from Adongolese forces in Otalo, and when he arrived in Pochalla, they arrested him. The colonial authority changed the nature of their strategies from military to politics, which was a soft war to fight. King Cham came to Pochalla in response to the British invitation with only a few bodyguards. He was not aware of the British dirty tactics to lure him away from his forces and they had secretly issued a warrant arrest for his arrest. King Cham, wearing his royal emblems, was immediately taken to Malakal. "He was imprisoned in Malakal for two years, and later was killed," Ojwok said. Evans-Pritchard (p. 97) wrote that King Cham-wara-Akello was executed before reaching his 18th birthday in 1934, but in 1927, Ocouk was brought back from Malakal to Pochalla after King Cham was killed. This confirmed that he was arrested in 1925 and killed in 1927.

King Cham-Wara-Akello was the youngest king to rule the kingdom since it was founded in the1500s. His kingship was disrupted by the British imperialist. Due to their political deception, King Cham paid the ultimate price for British revenge for the deaths of the soldiers who were killed in the battlefield in Juom by his father, the late King Akway Cham. When he was imprisoned in Malakal, King Cham was questioned about his father killing so many British soldiers in the battle of Juom. According to Ojwok, the British told Cham, your father killed so many British troops, but now you are going to die like them. The British wanted to know where King Akway Cham had received his guns from. They were upset not only for the lives they lost during the fight, but also for the humiliation such a defeat wrought. It proved that the British military superiority could not face the reality of the Anuaks' bravery. The Anuaks were very disciplined on the battlefield. It also showed that long before the British-Anuak war, King Akway invested heavily in national defence by acquiring guns from Ethiopia for self-defence.

Decades of organised military structure in the Anuak nation shocked the British when they encountered Anuak's military prowess. This could have been the first bloody war in the African continent that forced the British army to run away, leaving two commanding officers lying dead in the field (Evans-Pritchard, 1940). Fourteen years later, the British wanted to punish King Cham for his father's resistance to British invasion of Adongo in 1912. Evans-Pritchard (1940) asserted that it took fourteen years for the British to visit Otalo after they were defeated in the battle of Juom in 1912. The execution of Cham was direct revenge for the British soldiers who were killed by the anti-colonialism forces in Adongo known as Dhaldiim. In the same manner, Dhaliim forces were committed to remain free from British brutality in Africa! Ojwok explained that King Cham was sentenced to death by hanging! Prior to his execution, he was given time to say goodbye to his family, commoners, and farewell to the Anuak nation. "British gave Cham two choices: abdication of Ocuok or death. But Cham chose to be killed so that the royal emblem could go back to Otalo, the supremacy of the land," he said. As the crowned king, he communicated his last message like this: Cham wanted royal emblems to be taken back to his brothers in Otalo, according to Ojwok.

Sacrifice for The Nation

In Anuak politics, a leader may sacrifice his personal life for what he believes in. This showed that King Cham-wara-Akello preferred to die to preserve the dignity and supremacy of the Anuak kingdom. "King Cham was imprisoned for two years, but during those years he kept Ocuok with him in the prison," Ojwok said. But his precious life was prematurely taken by the British government because of his father's rejection of imperialism in their nation. As a result, an innocent king was brutally executed because the British wanted to control the Anuak kingdom. While Cham agreed to sacrifice his life, the British planned to keep Ocuok with them after his death. After he was killed, "Ocuok was kept in a store in Malakal. Surprisingly, the store was hit by lightning and thunder," said Ojwok.

Following warnings of natural disaster to the colonial officials, "the British transferred Ocuok to another store, yet the new store was hit by lightning and thunder again," he said. After execution of king Cham -wara-Akello in Malakal, there was heavy rain. Each time it rained, lighting and thunder hit the store where Ocuok was kept. The British people could not understand the divine kingship that came from the god of the river. It is imperative to remember that religion/god was introduced to the Greeks by the Egyptians. "Thus, when the Greek borrowed the Egyptian god, a real god in the full sense of the word, provided with all the moral perfections that stem from sedentary life, he could understand deity only by reducing him to the level of man," Diop stated.

This constant warning from the sky was a divine intervention. Anuaks believe that the king's authority comes directly from God, and no man has the right to take it away. More importantly, the royal emblems were properties of Ochudho who brought them from the river. Those emblems belonged to the god of the river and they could cause severe damage to the British if the Ocuok were to be taken to a museum in London.

The British feared for their lives so, they decided to return the royal emblem to the rightful owner in Otalo, according to Ojwok. "Ocuok caused trouble to the British people and that's why they brought it back," he said. King Cham sacrificed his life so that the royal emblem would come back to Otalo where it belongs! Ojwok said that the royal emblems generated revenues through coronations and other kingship functions. Consequently, when a prince wants to be crowned, he will pay fees for the coronation in Otalo, and those collected fees are used to provide services to the kingdom.

6

The British Council of Nobles

Council of nobles was formed to influence Anuak politics. The British were looking for ways to penalize the powerful king in the Adongo region. For them, killing one king was not enough. They wanted to reduce the level of military power in Otalo to nothing. The British wanted to reduce the powerful king in Otalo to the level of local kings who did not have power. Collins (1983) wrote that, in 1927, a district commissioner in Akobo, Major G.W. Tunnicliff refused to give the royal emblems back to Otalo. He was convinced by a group of princes from the Tung Goch clan that the royal emblems belonged to all kings, not one king. Moreover, members of the Tung Goch clan accused the late king Akway Cham of keeping Ocuok in Otalo. Tunnicliff allowed the crowning of new kings, which made many princes relieved from fear of losing their eligibility if the ban on coronation was not lifted. People from Tung Goch used this opportunity to support the British decision because they were afraid of losing the royal emblems to the descendants of King Akway Cham. Crowned kings and princes in the Tiernam region wanted the British to take the royal emblem and give it to them, instead of letting it go to Otalo.

Meanwhile, colonial officials deliberately planned to continue punishing kings in Otalo. According to the British authority, the powerful kings in Otalo were troublemakers. The British were unable to take Ocuok to the United Kingdom because of traditional power but weakening military power in Adongo was their primary goal in Anuak land. Thus, the British found ways to equalize all Anuak kings. According to their political strategy, the best way was to penalize the most powerful king in the kingdom. However, the establishment of the Anuak kingdom had to be abolished first. In this case, British commissioner Tunnicliff radically changed what Bacon proposed earlier as the best way to govern Anuak people under British authority in Sudan. Tunnicliff stated that his new proposal was to satisfy every descendant of Ochudho: It meant that any prince could be crowned and hold royal emblems for a certain time (Collins, 1983, p. 369). The British goal was to increase the number of powerless kings! It was the opposite of what late King Akway Cham did during his reign. After he defeated the two kings Olimi and Odiel, King Akway wanted to return kingship to its original position where the nation was ruled by one king at a time. According to him, defending the nation required collective defence to overcome future challenges.

On the other hand, the British knew that bringing the Anuak people under one ruler could be disastrous for their administration. They cited the unity of Adongolese people which led to the British defeat in Juom. For that reason, Tunnicliff's plan was to weaken the Anuak kingdom militarily and politically. In doing so, Collins writes, he created the council of nobles that allowed the coronation of many kings while rotating the emblems among them. The council of nobles removed Ocuok from one king while crowing another king, yearly. This was the third time royal emblems were rotated among the kings, but it was done through elections under the supervision of the British government in Sudan (Evans-Pritchard, p. 97).

Anuak Kings (1927-1935)

Even though two military invasions had failed, political invasions succeeded. In 1927, the British started administering Pochalla by annexing the Anuak nation to Sudan. From the first attempt in 1912, it took fifteen years for the

British to come to Anuak land (Evans-Pritchard, 1940). In Anuak kingship, the royal emblems are symbols of power and prestige, so every king wants to keep them. The British faced strong resistance to their attempts to control the emblems including from two appointed kings who ran away to Ethiopia with the royal emblems during their tenure.

The following kings were elected during the British tenure from 1927-1935:

1. In 1927, Nyang (Gora)Aganya was elected as a custodian of the emblems. But he took the royal emblems with him to Pinyudo, Ethiopia. Two years later, King Gora returned with the royal emblems to Sudan in 1929 (Evans-Pritchard, p. 97).

2. In 1929, after Gora returned to Sudan, he voluntarily gave Ocuok to Cham Metho.

3. In the same year, Akway Alal was elected.

4. In 1930, Cham Metho was elected as the holder of the emblems. According to Evans- Pritchard, King Cham Metho fled to Ethiopia with the emblems. In 1931, the Ethiopian government compelled him to return to Sudan in 1932. After Cham Metho returned from Ethiopia, Agwa Akwon was elected in 1932-1935 (Evans-Pritchard, p. 97). Evans-Pritchard admitted that "political difficulties continued to arise and led to the death in captivity of King Cham Akway in 1933 and the deportation of Cham Metho in 1934."

5. Finally, in 1935 after eight years of Ocuok rotation, King Cham-Wara-Achalla took them from King Agwa Akwon and returned royal emblems to Otalo. Evans-Pritchard reports: "When Cham-Wara-Achalla was frowned on by the government, the old men of Otalo thought that it was going to confiscate the emblems forever and they invested all the young sons of nobles in the vicinity," he said. He disagreed with the British involvement in the Anuak kingdom. He said it was British ignorance that led them to appoint kings in a political system they did not understand. To restore the legacy of his younger brother, Cham-Wara-Akello, who was killed by the British, King Cham-Wara-Achalla took the royal emblems back to Otalo.

In this new political development, another son of late king Akway Cham led the Third Dynasty up to the current time. From the Second Dynasty to Third Dynasty, the Tung Goch Royal lineage lost ownership of the royal emblems forever. According to King Cham, sacrifice made by the Adongolese people was the reason they still maintained Ocuok. First, in 1910, Akway Cham took the royal emblems from King Olimi Aganya. He kept them in Otalo until his death in 1920. Second, British arrested King Cham-wara-Akello and took him to Malakal in 1925. Two years later, he was executed by British authorities in Malakal. It is vital for the readers to know how long the royal emblems have stayed in Otalo: From 1910-1925, Ocuok was in Otalo for 15 years. Furthermore, King Cham-Wara-Achalla took them from King Agwa Akwon in 1935 and they have been sitting permanently in Otalo since.

It was the bravery of Cham-Wara-Achalla to defy British rules. He strongly warned the British of another war should they dare follow him to Otalo for the royal emblems (Collins, 1983). Collins asserts that Adongo's people were ready to fight Commissioner Tunnicliffe, who controlled the council of nobles temporarily in the Anuak Kingdom. "On another occasion, the holder of the emblems simply retired to the Adongo region and challenged Tunnicliffe to come and get them, defended as they were by some 600-armed followers," Collins said.

Retention of Ocuok in Otalo was an honour for which every Adongolese man fought. It was the capital of the Anuak kingdom since 1910. Keeping the royal emblems in Otalo is a permanent reminder to the Adongolese people of their national heroes! The royal emblem is a symbol of unity, power, and pride of the Anuak people. Consequently, those royal emblems deserved to be kept in the palace of the king of kings who united the Anuak nation. From internal rivalries to British-Anuak war in 1912, Adongo's people learned that perseverance was a panacea to overcome obstacles to achieve freedom and justice. Overall, the Adongolese people dealt with every trial successfully from one generation to another.

King Cham-Wara-Achalla (1935-1940)

Cham-Wara-Akello, a successor of great king Akway Cham, prepared his brothers for future leadership. After his coronation, he had the legitimate authority to crown Cham-Wara-Achalla and other princes, according to King Akway Agada in an interview. Meanwhile, the youngest king remained in

Otalo as the head of the nation (Evans-Pritchard, 1940). Before the British interfered in Anuak royal affairs in 1927, the king was the only holder of the royal emblems. Equally important to note that kingship was indivisible, so whoever held the emblems was the king in the nation.

However, the death of the great king and execution of his son by the British changed the royal order. In the time of Akway Cham's reign after he defeated king Olimi and King Odiel, he held emblems for almost two decades. Besides, King Akway was planning to ban more princes from coronation so that there would be one king at a time for the whole tribe. His untimely death left his plan unfinished. Seven years after king Akway died, the British became directly involved in Anuak politics and changed his vision for a unified kingdom to something else. After Cham-Wara-Akello was executed, British prevented royal emblems from returning to Otalo, and the British commissioner in Akobo created a council of nobles to appoint Anuaks kings (Evans-Pritchard, P-97). While some of the princes and kings agreed with the British intervention into the affairs of the kingdom, Cham-Wara-Achalla strongly opposed them. He saw the British plan as an attempt to weaken the Anuak kingdom by equalizing every crown and humiliating of the king in Otalo who was more powerful than the others.

It was almost a decade of the emblems circulating among British-appointed kings (Evans-Pritchard, 1940). Cham, in 1935, violated British rule by coming from Otalo and taking royal emblems from King Agwa Akwon (Collins,1983). King Cham left with the royal emblems and the British did not pursue him due to fear of another war with the Anuak people in Adongo. King Cham was ready to engage with the British authority if they came to Otalo to take those emblems again! Due to King Cham's bravery, Ocuok returned to Otalo after being under British control for eight years.

Cham-wara-Achalla became the king in Otalo in 1935. Soon after, he reorganized the Adongolese military. Since the late king was imprisoned in Malakal and executed, there was no king in Otalo, but the acting king remained in charge. Before Cham came to power, there was security concerns in the Tiernam region in the south east of the Olimi Triangle on the border with the Suri people (Kacipo) and Suk-Suka in Ethiopia (Collins, 1983). Olimi Akwon was an Anuak king who lived at Okwa in Tiernam state. To resolve the troubles among the neighbouring tribes—Murle, Suri, and Suk-Suka—King Olimi exercised his political power to find a solution for the problems. As the king in the region, Olimi led a combined force of Anuak and Murle to attack Kacipo and capture some individuals who hid among their people. But the Kacipo community stood up and supported the troublemakers. Unfortunately, it turned to heavy fighting and King Olimi's forces defeated Kacipo and chased them far away, according to Collins.

Another reason for the attack was an attempt to stop the Kacipo ambushing Anuak people on the road between gold mining camps. Similarly, Murle and Kacipo had been engaging in cattle rustling. Dealing with the pastoralist neighbours was not an easy task. Efforts of the king to maintain peace and security between Murle and Kacipo people were not recognized by the warring parties. This suggested that King Olimi used diplomacy and military means to solve inter-tribal conflicts. Both tribes were acephalous or people without organized political systems. Paradoxically, Olimi paid the ultimate price for his peace-loving mission! King Olimi Akwon was assassinated by Kacipo men, who ambushed him (Collins, 1983).

Immediately, the Anuak retaliated for the killing of the king. Both Tiernamese Anuaks and Murle people from Boma joined in against the Kacipo. Unlike the previous attack, this mission involved Ethiopian forces who came to the Kacipo's aid. According to Collins, with their help, the Anuaks and Murles were defeated (Collins, 1983). As a result of the higher casualties, Anuak people turned against the Murle for creating problems in the region. The Murle often stole cattle from the neighbouring tribes. During Olimi's reign, he tried to broker peace in the region, but it was difficult dealing with anarchists and pastoralist communities in South Sudan. The Anuak community was very disappointed to lose the crowned king. Later, Cham-wara-Achalla took personal responsibility to restore law and order in the Olimi Triangle.

Anarchy in the Olimi Triangle

King Olimi Akwon was a prominent leader in the Tiernam region, and his assassination shocked the Anuak kingdom. Collins (1983) stated that at the time of Olimi's death, his brother, Agwa Akwon, was the holder of the emblem, but he could not do anything without risking punishment from British authorities. On the other hand, King Cham-wara-Achalla was a risk-taker who did not care about the British rule. He knew that British were controlling the kingdom while the Anuak people were dying. King Cham was a patriotic leader who wanted to save the lives of his people, wherever they lived. He believed that nobody could take the lives of Anuak people with impunity. Any king in Otalo was a national leader who dealt with security threats irrespective of location. The goal was to secure and protect the Anuak people from all foreign aggressors.

When Anuaks from Tiernam were defeated by Ethiopian forces, they already drove Kacipo people into the villages of Suk-Suka people, their neighbouring tribe in Southern Ethiopia. Now, King Cham-wara-Achalla led Adongolese forces to attack Suk-Suka, according to King Akway Agada . King Cham attacked Suk-Suka's stronghold and destroyed their villages. "After Cham took power, he went to Suk-Suka with young men; many people thought that King Cham would not bring anything, or he would not win the war," King Akway said. Amazingly, King Cham-Wara-Achalla and his young men did a tremendous job. King Akway stated: "Surprisingly, during the fighting, Adongolese forces defeated Suk-Suka and they brought children and cattle together. When they arrived in Otalo, King Cham named his forces Kalngo." In other words, what seemed impossible earlier by the Tiernamese forces was winnable to the Adongolese warriors. Those young men who fought in the Suk-Suka battle were Bongkido Obitch Kwach, Ogala Odol, and Obudo Gak-Maai, to mention a few veterans of that war.

The name **kalngo**, means what will they bring? Kalngo became the name of the battalion of young men who fought bravely in Suk-Suka: It was an ironic statement in response to the joke made about what would the young men bring! Following the attack in Suk-Suka, the Ethiopian government intervened to rescue Suk-Suka people who were captured during the war to be taken back to their homes. The Ethiopian government complained to the colonial government in Khartoum. "Ethiopians complained to the British about the attack and the British told King Cham-Wara-Achalla to take the captured Suk-Suka people back to Ethiopia," King Akway said. Through diplomatic coordination between the British and the Ethiopian governments, eventually the captured people were returned to their homes in Suk-Suka's villages in Southern Ethiopia. According to Evans-Pritchard, Olimi Aganya was killed during his foreign expedition. After his death, another king from the same clan was also killed far away from his home. King Olimi Aganya and King Olimi Akwon, all were from one clan and they lived in the same region.

7

The British and Ethiopian Coalition

Diplomatic relations between Ethiopia and British government since 1902 ruined the Anuak nation. The priority of Anglo-Egyptian government in Sudan was to weaken and destroy the Anuak people. Through alliance with the Ethiopian government, both countries teamed up to weaken Anuak political system, which was the strongest political institution in Africa during the colonization period. In their relations, the Ethiopian government protected its Suk-suka and Suri citizens—Ethiopian tribes who lived in the Olimi Triangle bordered by Anuak in Tiernam state. But the British betrayed the Anuak people in Sudan. When King Olimi Akwon was assassinated by Ethiopian Suri men or Kacipo people, the British did not investigate. For that reason, the Anuak people took responsibility and responded.

However, when Anuaks used military means to resolve the situation in the Olimi Triangle, the British authorities stepped in to punish the Anuak leaders. Their hatred of the Anuak people proved that victims could be punished for self-preservation! For the British and Ethiopians, the lives of the Anuak people did not matter. Both countries were happy to wipe out the Anuak people. Hence, it was considered a serious crime when the Anuaks used force in self-defence. King Akway told me, the colonial government in Khartoum had threatened King Cham-Wara-Achalla to return captured cattle, goats, and sheep to Suk-Suka people in Ethiopia. However, the cause of the attack on Suk-Suka was not addressed by the British, who were not interested in protecting the Anuak. Their job was to make the Anuak vulnerable or defenceless in their dealings with Ethiopians, Nuer, Murle, Suri and Suk-Suka. The action of the Anglo-Egyptian government to weaken the power of the Anuak king was a deliberate attempt to prevent Anuak defending themselves (Evans-Pritchard,1940, p. 104-105).

During the British rule in Sudan, their support was always for those who crossed into Anuak land. The 1902 agreement signed by the British and Ethiopian kingdom was the starting point of destroying the independence of the Anuak nation. The signatories of the agreement made sure that Anuaks were weakened and subdued by other nations. In fact, colonialism in Africa preached false ideologies to the African people. For instance, the original builders of civilization were black Egyptians, the Luo people to be precise, not whites according to Diop. In the nineteenth century, the very Europeans who were taught in Egypt by black scholars were now claiming that Africans were incapable of building states. The path of civilization traced from blacks to whites! Furthermore, Europeans found African civilization in Egypt and they adopted it from African/Luo (Onyala, 2019). The British could not believe what they saw in the Anuak kingdom. There they found a functional government with strong political institutions and a national army capable of defeating the British forces at the Battle of Juom (Evans-Pritchard, 1940).

This was evidence of African states that the British did not want to admit! Note that the Anuak people did not fit into the Western definition of "**stateless nations**". However, Europeans had to destroy any existence of states in Africa to deceive blacks about whites' superiority and civilization. Due to racial stereotypes, white people believed that their mission was to elevate uncivilized Africans from backwardness. Without a doubt, blacks taught civilization to whites and they adapted the culture of blacks and religion (Diop,1989). It showed that Europeans repackaged the Anu religion to teach it the younger generation of Anu people. Nothing new! The destruction of the Anuak nation proved that African people were capable of building states long before the Europeans arrived. Overall, it was a strange mission to teach Africans to believe in white man's religion was a reverse in the course of history. First, it was the Luo people who introduced religion to Greeks/whites (Diop, 1989). For those Europeans who received their education in Egypt, to claim that they were the ones who civilized black people was a lie. Those lies were created by colonial masters. Later, the British people came face to face with reality! Their political agreement with Emperor Menelik crushed Anuak power through political manoeuvring in both Ethiopia and Sudan (Collins, 1983). It was too powerful for one empire to conquer. The impact of the British agreement with the Ethiopian kingdom affected Anuaks from 1902 until the present and possibly for years to come.

The British propaganda was malicious, particularly after the Anuak people defeated them in the battle of Juom. Nevertheless, the British continued their political fight by disseminating false information about the Anuak people internationally. To build a successful empire or imperialism in Africa, British considered the anti-colonial nation the worst enemy of Western civilization. Any political establishment in Africa that contradicted European views was deemed an outrage to White supremacy. The following statement was the best British propaganda launched to destroy the reputation of the Anuak people:

> *There is a tribe called Anuak living in the South Eastern Sudan and Western Ethiopian frontier, they were born trained. Therefore, do not give them power and education, if you do, they will be more powerful than you*
> —**Anglo-Egyptian Sudan political ads.**

The above quote was posted in Port Sudan for every European traveller to see how dangerous Anuak people were in rejecting colonialism. This political propaganda was meant to isolate the Anuak people from their peaceful neighbours—the Oromo people. Soon after, the relationship between the Oromo people and the Anuaks deteriorated and trading ceased between the two nations. The Oromo were threatened to stop selling guns and ammunition to the Anuak people.

Due to British campaign, the Anuaks ran out of ammunition and they were left with no other supply lines. The Anglo-Egyptian policies in Sudan towards the Anuaks proved disastrous and damaging for every aspect of their lives. Moreover, the British engaged in a proxy war by favouring tribes that were traditional enemies of the Anuak nation. Since the British arrival in South Sudan, they learned that Murles often went to Anuak villages to steal cattle and kidnap children. The Murle people have cattle rustled for nearly a century in Anuak, Nuer, Dinka, Kacipo, Jie and other tribes of Equatoria region. According to Evans-Pritchard (1940, p. 20) the government of Anglo-Egyptian Sudan and Ethiopian government took cattle from the Anuak people in Ciro/Akobo and Nyikani regions as a penalty for counter-raiding the Murle.

Despite these criminal activities by the Murle, the British did not bother to take action, yet were ready to punish Anuaks. Evans-Pritchard (1940) revealed that Anglo-Egyptian government forcefully seized about 300 cattle from Ciro and Nyikani regions. In the same manner, the Ethiopian government took cattle from the Anuak people in Wicnam, Koc, and Pinykoaa (Evans-Pritchard, p. 20-21). This gives some insight into what the Anuak people went through during the British colonial rule in Sudan. There was unpublished information about the Anuak people in Sudanese government's files according to Evans-Pritchard. Yet, the contents remained unknown to the Anuak people until now.

Extensive evidence showed that the British deliberately destroyed the Anuak nation. The diplomatic protest in Addis Ababa resulted in restricting gun sales between Anuak and Oromo in the borderlands (Collins, 1983). Meanwhile, British government curtailed, and sanctioned companies involved in what they called "illegal arms traffic in Ethiopia".

It appeared the most effective strategy that not only blocked Anuaks from buying guns and ammunition from Ethiopia, but also destroyed the relationship between Anuaks and the Oromo people. Eventually, the diplomatic protest in Addis Ababa convinced Austria to act. Collins (1983) writes that after the protest in Ethiopia, abandoned rifles that were purchased in larger numbers by the European and American merchants. As a result, gun shipments through Djibouti were stopped. According to Collins, British estimated that

Anuak people had 10,000 guns at that time, making it difficult for the British to disarm them or penetrate their country easily. Since their defeat, the British led destructive campaigns to weaken and destroy the Anuak people diplomatically because they rejected colonization.

Anuak Political Achievements

King Cham- Wara- Achalla's greatest achievements was the return of the royal emblems to Otalo from King Agwa Akwon, who was appointed by the British. Cham-Wara-Achalla was not on the list of the successors that were chosen by the King, according to King Akway. However, he jumped into royal duty to confront the British. He exhibited confidence and strength in doing so and was successful. During the reign of late King Cham-Wara-Akello, he crowned a few princes including Gillo-Wara-Orow, Cham-Wara-Achalla, Metho-Wara-Adew, Aballa Nguu and Metho-Wara-Winyicenthoa. After their coronations, they went to stay in the villages of their mothers, or to live with their maternal relatives in other places. It was the brilliant idea of Cham-Wara-Akello to invest in three of his half-brothers and two cousins with the royal emblems to maintain kingship in case he died prematurely. In fact, those crowned kings later took responsibility in the kingdom. As a rule, after the official coronation was completed in Otalo, a newly crowned king would go to his residency. In less than a week after Cham-Wara-Achalla's coronation, he moved to Obuodi to live with his maternal relatives: people of the Ogaa Clan in Obuodi, who supported Cham because his older brother, Odol Aballa Gur-Boko, was already living there.

However, after the confirmation of Cham-Wara-Akello's death, Cham-Wara-Achalla came from Obuodi where he was already a king and he took power in Otalo. He installed himself as King in Otalo. King Cham took the position of his half-brother who was the heir to the throne in Otalo, according to the will of their father, King Akway Cham. Now, Gillo-Wara-Orow, who was successor, had to wait longer. Gillo was a patient individual and humble king. So, he did not force his way to the throne in Otalo because such action would cost innocent lives. He did not believe in past traditions in which many princes murdered their own brothers for power. Gillo continued to live in the Ojwa region with his maternal uncles. Later when King Cham-Wara-Achalla died of natural causes, Gillo took power in the headquarters. Unfortunately, in less than a year in the office, King Gillo was assassinated by his own half-brother, Agole Akway, in 1941. His youngest half-brother, Agada Akway Cham took the kingship in 1942, according to King Akway Agada.

Gillo was the victim of his two ambitious half-brothers—Cham-Wara-Achalla and Agole-Winyobak. They planned to be kings whether they were in the royal line or not. But each had plans to seize power at different times and by different means. First, Cham took Gillo's position when it was his turn to be king. Secondly, in less than a year on the throne, Agole-Winyobak assassinated him. "When Gillo was king, one day youths were dancing traditional music or Bul, prince Agole Akway stole into the crowd and shot the king while he watched the dancers. Agole ran away as soon as he fired the shot and proclaimed, he has killed Gillo-Wara-Orow," King Akway said. However, Gillo did not die instantly and called on the Adongolese people not to fight one another. "Gillo said, 'my brother attempted to kill me, but he was shooting himself in the arm', this is an Anuak proverb, which means a person who kills his brother destroys his own family," King Akway explained.

In Gillo's last speech, he predicted that his brother who had attempted to kill him would never sit on the royal throne. He said that when he died, advisers would go to Akobo and bring his younger brother Agada-War-Dikang to assume the throne in Otalo. Assassinations of crowned kings ended in the Second Dynasty. But in the Third Dynasty, Agem (revolution or coup) in the kingdom could not be ignored as it took people back to the previous century of continuous plots and murders. The monarchy was at its highest development which would not tolerate violence of the past centuries. Therefore, the assassination of Gillo required serious measures to hold the perpetrator accountable. In 1910, assassination for kingship was abolished. It had been three decades since King Akway Cham seized the royal emblems from King Olimi and defended them when King Odiel Kwot attacked him in Otalo to take the royal emblems by force (Evans-Pritchard, 1940). That was the end of assassinating an incumbent king for a new king to take over. For that reason, most people in Adongo region supported King Agada -War-Dikang to prevent prince Agole-Winyobak from coming to power through violence.

King Agada Akway Cham (1942-2000)

After the death of King Gillo-War-Orow, King Agada was crowned in Otalo. King Agada was determined to restore law and order in the Anuak kingdom. One of his first tasks was to ensure that other tribes did not expand into Anuak land.

Liberation of Angela in Rwanye State from Nuer Invasion

In 1975, Nuer people invaded Angela which was aggressively resisted by the Anuak. They fought invaders, but they were overwhelmed. As a result, they tactically withdrew from the area and the Nuer advanced to secure Angela. According to Ochalla, Angela's residents fought the Nuer for five days before they took the wounded, women and children to safety.

Jor state, which bordered the Rwanye region, reinforced the people of Angela, followed by people from the Baat Gillo region to help the Angela resistance. During that period, Jor became the headquarters for people from different regions to prepare for another offensive against the Nuer in Anglea. "People came from Gony, Olaw, Centhoa, Tuo, Arieth, Cham, Teedo and Owelo," Ochalla said. These collective efforts to push the Nuer out of Angela's territory failed.

Gol was a place where people of Angela stayed in the dry season and worked on summer farms. The Anuak coalition forces attacked the Nuer in the summer of 1978, known as the battle of Gol. It was a bloody war. The Anuak forces pushed the enemy towards the river, isolating them from the rest of the Nuer population. The Nuer realized the plan was dangerous and aimed to kill everyone on the battlefield. The Nuer who could not swim and were more likely to drown in the river. Nevertheless, they had few options available: the Nuer avoided positioning themselves where they would be directed by the Anuak fighters. Instead, they forcefully opened their way in the opposite direction. This led to higher casualties when they penetrated through the Anuak forces to avoid being trapped and pushed toward the river. It was the bloodiest war fought in Angela since its invasion. The Nuers fought in a suicidal fashion to open the way with hundreds were killed. "This time the

Nuer defeated Anuaks in the fight," Ochalla said. After that fight, Nuers held Angela for a year before they were defeated once and for all.

Ochalla disclosed how the enemy was defeated in the last battle of Angela a year later. He was among the forces that recaptured Angela. According to Ochalla, he joined people of Olaw. "Nuers wanted land and fish in Angela," he said. The motive of the Nuers in Angela was to take the land. He asserted that all lakes and rivers in Rwanye state were full of fish! Therefore, the Nuers' planned to take Anuak land, piece by piece. Their strategy was simple and clear: Nuers would come to Anuak land during peace between the two communities and would pretend to settle peacefully. However, Nuers would keep coming in large numbers and overstay their welcome which was only for the dry season. Later when the Nuers outnumbered the Anuak residents in a village, they would start attacking them. This is what happened in Angela village. They have been using similar strategies for the past 171 years (1850-2021).

Great leaders of Anuak history are remembered for their bravery and determination! The people of Angela were determined not to leave their ancestral land to the Nuer people.

They fought the Nuers many times. Eventually, people of Angela were supported by neighbouring regions, Jor and Baat Gillo. This commitment to Angela liberation was another step in reaching the most influential king in the Anuak nation, King Agada Akway.

Ojill Omot Okwom, Chief of Jor, was determined to win the war in Angela no matter how long it took. Ojill and Omot Oman, an acting chief of Angela, travelled to the Adongo region together to seek military support from King Agada Akway in Otalo. Both leaders played important roles in Anuak politics, according to Ochalla. "Omot Oman went to King Agada in Otalo. Telling him that Angela was about to be lost to Nuer. Omot said he needed help: military power and ammunition," Ochalla said.

When Ojill and his delegation arrived in Otalo, they briefed King Agada Akway. They explained what happened in Angela and the endless wars they fought against the Nuer. "Ojill, the chief of Jor, went to Otalo to ask King Agada for military support," King Akway said. Otalo was always ready to defend and protect the Anuak people from foreign aggression since the Second Dynasty. During a consultation with other leaders in the nation for more military offensive, the Nuer believed that Angela was gone; they celebrated victory.

King Agada and The Liberation of Angela

Evans-Pritchard (p. 104) observed: "[The king in Adongo] also became the leader of the Anuaks against the Nuer and Murle and organized raiding expeditions against them." After the meeting with the king regarding insecurity in Angela, King Agada agreed to provide reinforcements and made a commitment to liberate Angela! Thus, he provided ammunition and he sent sixty military personnel from the Adongolese royal forces to lead the Angela operation effectively.

He appointed three leaders to command the special royal force: Agwa Nyang (Akwaynyyang Nyiwatcua) to command twenty people from Otego division, Akway Obitch led twenty people from Otalo division, and Otor Nyigwo commanded another twenty from Aleo division, according to King Akway. Those three leaders were known for their military success in battlefields. "King Agada gave sixty Adongolese military personnel, a group of prominent snipers to support Angela liberation," King Akway stated. Those sixty boosted the morale of the Anuak people. They were well equipped and provided more ammunition to the rest of the fighters. The crack team joined Anuaks from different regions. One of the fighters stated that the Anuaks attacked Angela early one morning and Nuers were defeated! During the attack, a famous Nuer magician woman, Nyachay, was killed. "Nuer people ran away and left behind cattle, sheep, and goats," King Akway reported. As Nuers dispersed, many of their cattle were left behind.

"Angela's liberation took less than thirty minutes," said Ochalla. Nuer people did not take anything: Cows, goats, sheep, and other valuable belongings. When they saw Anuaks were taking their cattle, they came back to get them. "However, Adongolese people fought to prevent the Nuers from taking the cattle," according to Ochalla. The Adongolese royal force lined up between the Anuaks, who carried hundreds of cattle, and blocked the enemy preventing them from getting their cows back, he said. With the Adongolese military power, Angela fell easily! "The last war in Angela was fought on 11

November 1979; it was the end of Angela's occupation," Ochalla said. After the defeat of Nuer, they never came back to Angela again. It has been forty-two years (1979-2021) since the Nuer people were defeated by collective defence. Angela remains in the hands of the Anuak people today.

King Agada Finalizes Obuodi Payment

Another King Agada's achievement was to finalize a land deal. Obuodi is in the Adongo region. It pledged its allegiance to the supreme king in Otalo, the capital of the Adongo region. Obuodi became an Adongolese territory during King Cham-Winy-Nyijuu's reign before the acquisition of firearms in 1880. "Obuodi became part of Adongo when Cham-Winy-Nyijuu was the king and when he died, he passed it on to his son, Akway Tor, or King Akway-Wara-Cham," King Akway Agada said. The landowner of Obuodi sold it to King Cham for four Dimuy: Strings of beads normally used for bride-wealth and in the agreement, half of the price was paid to the seller immediately. According to their agreement, the full price of the land was four Dimuys, a price that was equivalent to full payment for bride-wealth at that time. The rest of the payments were paid later by King Agada Akway to complete the Obuodi payment, he said. In other words, the grandson of Cham-Winy-Nyijuu made the last payments. "Aballa-War-Guno Obaang went to king Ochudho-War- Odol to get the rest of the payments. He was told to go to King Agada for the payment. Aballa came to King Agada and the two remaining Dimuys were paid to him," King Akway explained. In modern times, when a person purchased a piece of land, it became the property of the buyer. In this case, Obuodi became the Adongolese land marking the border between Adongo and Tiernam states in the Anuak federation.

8

Europeans in Ethiopia and Sudan

Colonization of Africa by European powers falsely claimed to "civilize Africans" from barbarism! In their distorted view, Europeans were responsible for the civilization of African people. The term to civilize Africans from their backwardness does not make sense to black people when studying the origin of civilization. Blacks started civilization in Egypt while whites still lived in deep barbaric conditions in Europe. Diop (1989, p. 22) asserts that by 4245 BC Blacks in Egypt had invented a calendar, which took thousands of years to develop. Furthermore, he states that civilization started in Africa not in Europe. Above all, it was the work of Luo people that elevated all human race from primitivity and barbarism. It began in every field: religion, kingship, politics, agriculture and later it expanded beyond Egypt's borders. As a centre of knowledge, all races learned, adapted, or stole wealth from the Egyptian culture. The pattern of civilization is still undeniable: It moved from ancient Egyptians to Greeks and Romans. As Anu people lay the foundation of civilization, British had no legitimate reason to invade Anuaks. The Turks, Greeks, French, and British came to Egypt in Africa to learn how powerful the Kush kingdom was and they copied its civilized governance. But later, black power declined and white stepped up to dominate the world (Diop, 1989).

An agreement to divide Anuak people into two countries—Ethiopia and Sudan—was signed in 1902 by Ethiopian Emperor Menelik and Anglo-Egyptian Sudan (Collins, 1983). The agreement destroyed independence of the Anuak country. In addition, the agreement between the two parties ignored the rights of the Anuak people in their own land. It was ignorance of the Ethiopians and the British to decide the fate of the Anuaks without their knowledge. As a reminder, Anu and Anuak are the same people. Yet, Europeans omitted two letters intentionally to make Anu people different from Anuaks. It was European manipulation that distorted the identity of one tribe and made them look different. The ancestors of those people invented mathematics, astronomy, sciences, arts, religion, agriculture, social organizations, medicine, writing and architecture (Diop, p. 234). The Anu people were a fountain source for Greeks knowledge in politics and religion since the twelfth dynasty of the Kush kingdom according to Diop. This showed that European political organizations were made from Egyptians' civilization and kingship.

The Ethiopian and Anglo-Egyptian Sudan signed the agreement to give Gambella to the Ethiopian kingdom. But none of the invaders knew the geographical location of Gambella that bordered with Western Ethiopia (Collins, 1983). The signatories of the agreement not only lived far away from the Anuak country but did not know Anuak people were not Ethiopians. In fact, Anuak people are Luos! Culturally and linguistically, Anuak people are different from Ethiopian highlanders: Oromo, Amhara, and Tigray. Hence, the Ethiopian and British who decided their fate committed political genocide that affected the lives of the Anuak people for 119 years (1902-2021). It was a genuine manipulation by the British to appease Emperor Menelik of Ethiopia, while they were planning to fight with a Sudanese leader Khalifa Abd Allahi in Sudan (Collins, 1983). The purpose of the agreement was to secure Menelik's neutrality in the upcoming conflict with the Sudanese, according to Collins. The division of Anuaks into Ethiopia and Sudan was done without consultation.

European Manipulation

The division of Anuak people took place on 15 May 1902 through an agreement between Emperor Menelik and Anglo-Egyptian Sudan (Collins, 1983). This is the best example of how Africa was broken into pieces by European empires. Africa's boundaries drawn by the colonial governments were artificial European creations with no regard for African nation-states, according to Kevin.

Due to racial stereotypes, Europeans disregarded pre-colonial states in the African continent (Kevin, 2012, p. 433). The plan was to deny any existing states in Africa to prove that Africans were uncivilized, or they did not have political systems that existed before Europeans arrived in Africa. As a result, people with different languages, political systems and cultures were put together in one country for European interests, according to Kevin. Anuak people were victims of this policy! They lived in their own independent kingdom and were never a part of the Ethiopian kingdom. Their language, political systems, culture and even landscapes had nothing in common with the Ethiopian people in the highlands.

British appeasement with the Ethiopian government ended the independence of the Anuak people in their own country. It was fragmented and systems dismantled. From the First Dynasty in the fifteenth century to the beginning of the Second Dynasty in the 1900s, Anuak people have been living independently in their country. It was the British who divided them in two countries—Ethiopia and Sudan. It was absurd for the British to assume that Gambella region (Openo region) was part of Ethiopia. It belonged to the Anuak nation! The international boundary between Ethiopia and Paanywaa was known to the neighbouring tribes: Oromo and Anuak. The two nations are naturally demarcated by the mountain. To understand it better, Ethiopian people lived on the top of the mountain while Anuaks lived at the bottom of it. This natural boundary is called **Kewa-kidi** in Anuak language which means our boundary is mountain (Ethiopian escarpment). Consequently, it was a great mistake for the British government to give Anuak land to Ethiopia while giving the other portion to Sudan. As mentioned earlier, Anuak people have never been part of the Ethiopian kingdom, they had sovereign rights in their own kingdom. Prior to their division, the Anuak people had their political systems that dated back fifteen centuries (Collins, 1983). Their governments were led by headmen/chiefs in most parts of the country, but fewer regions/states were governed by kings. Nevertheless, there were no Ethiopian authorities in Anuak land, nor did their government exist anywhere in the Anuak nation (Evans-Pritchard, 1940).

Evidence of the agreement revealed the destruction caused by British and Ethiopian governments after they signed an agreement that destroyed one of the oldest African states: Paanywaa. The Anuak people built a kingdom, which had lived from ancient times to modern times! It took time for the British people to know the truth about the Anuak people. In 1921, after a British officer visited Otalo and Pochalla, he realized that Anuak country was an independent state. It was shocking to the British people to know that the Ethiopian government was not present anywhere in the Anuak land according to Evans-Pritchard. Eventually, the British admitted that there were no Ethiopian authorities in Anuak land (Evans-Pritchard, 1940). With this truth it became irrefutable ignorance that the British colonial government should claim that Anuaks were Ethiopians. The British have repeated this mistake in many other African nations because they did not bother to know the facts. The British falsely claimed the Anuak as Ethiopian and this was dishonest! More importantly, it was the racist policy of European governments to decide where some tribes belonged by creating maps that did not exist before their arrival in Africa (Kevin, 2012, p. 433). Even though Africans identified where they belonged and where their boundaries with other nations lay, their knowledge was completely ignored by the colonial powers. Anuak people knew their geographical locations better than the colonial powers who divided their land into pieces. European powers crumbled African nations among themselves to take Africa's resources to enrich their countries in Europe (Kevin, 2012).

Imperialists' Exploitation of Africa's Natural Resources

The European imperialists divided African countries among themselves to loot, pillage, and control markets in Africa (Kevin, 2012, p. 312). Furthermore, European presence in Africa was brutal for the African people. They created inhumane conditions for African people. Without shame, integrity or justice, these nations falsely claimed that they were civilizing black people in the continent. The opposite is true. Europeans enslaved Africans! These acts were far away from humane and certainly not civilized. Europeans found Africans living in peace when they came to Egypt. According to Diop, blacks discovered iron and made gunpowder long before the whites. Evans-Pritchard confirmed that Othieno was a famous man in Anuak society for his expertise in metal work. According to him, Othieno made spears called Dem and dancing bells from the iron. Diop (1989) claims white nations discovered iron after it was known to blacks and made ships out of it. This, technically, new development enabled Europeans to travel far distances, which led to discovery of the new world (Diop, 1989). In the fifteenth century the change in power due to technical advancement, gave Europeans the upper hand to control and dominate blacks. That was the time power shifted from blacks to whites! Thus, Europeans were interested in African lands and resources. It was a lucrative business for the European companies that produced "cloth, clothing, alcohol, guns and metal manufactured goods, all poured into the African continent in search of new markets (Kevin, 2012, p. 312).

To achieve their goals in Africa, Europeans turned African people against one another, exploiting traditional rivalries among the African nations, according to Kevin. As Europeans took sides in African tribal conflicts, the British pursued Anuak people. They were supporting the Nuer, Anuak's traditional enemy. In the same manner, the British took cattle from the Anuaks and gave them to Murle people as a penalty (Evans-Pritchard, 1940). Worst of all, the British brought Ethiopians to Anuak country. It clearly showed that the British promoted enmity among the Africans to achieve their goals. The British used the divide and conquered strategy to weaken the stronger tribes, enabling the colonization of the other tribes.

Due to their deception, some African rulers made treaties with the Europeans to protect themselves from their fellow Africans (Kevin, 2012, p. 313). However, these alliances proved only temporary as their friendships did not last peacefully. Kevin asserted: "It was only when those traditional African enemies had been brutally conquered that the full implication of European 'protection' became clear." According to him, no African leaders knowingly or willingly signed away the sovereignty of their nations (Kevin, 2012). But through political manipulation, Europeans believed that Africans sold their land to them. Moreover, when Europeans realized that there were immense resources in Africa, almost every country in Europe came to loot African resources (Kevin, 2012). They used force to wipe out African people from their fertile land to make room for European farmers. Kevin (2012) wrote: "In the 1870s and 1880s, however, African armies were rapidly overtaken by advances in European weaponry. First came the breech-loading repeater rifle, to be followed by the maxim-gun in 1889, the world's first highly mobile modern machine-gun."

Those deadly weapons were used to kill Africans to force them to vacate their lands for European settlers. To colonize African nations more effectively, Europeans held a conference that determined the fate of African nations. "The Berlin conference held in 1884-1885 agreed that European claims to any part of Africa would only be recognized by other European governments if they were effectively occupied by that particular European power," Kevin wrote. Therefore, this agreement allowed the European countries to pursue their national interests via exploitation of Africa's natural resources. Through political control, Africans were no longer free in their own countries. Eventually, Africans participated in European wars that did not benefit them in any way but only served the interests of their colonial masters. Greed to control wealth in Africa led some European countries to fight each other either to maintain, or to remove another European colonizer from the African nation it previously occupied (Kevin, 2012).

To understand the destruction caused by the European land-grabbers, it is crucial to look at colonial powers in North and East Africa and the causes of fighting for territorial control. For example, from August to September 1940, Italian forces occupied British Somaliland in Somalia. At the same time, Italians invaded the British military base in Libya (Kevin, 2012, p. 382). In response to the Italian invasion, in December 1940, British attacked the Italian forces and pushed them back into Libya, far from their military base. In January 1941, the British invaded Ethiopia to push Italian forces out of Addis Ababa, Ethiopia. Emperor Haile Selassie was brought from the United Kingdom through Southern Sudan to lead the Ethiopian forces. But those

Ethiopian armies were scattered throughout the country due to their defeat by the Italian forces (Kevin, 2012, p. 382). Ethiopia was reinforced by its British allies. The British brought in African troops from Nigeria, Ghana, Sudan, and Sierra Leone, meanwhile the French brought another African army from Congo to fight in Ethiopia, according to Kevin. As a result of this military coalition, Addis Ababa was captured in May 1941 and Emperor Haile Selassie, who had been in exile for five years, reclaimed his throne (Kevin, 2012). This showed that the early liberation of Ethiopia from Italian rule was the British plan to get rid of its competitor in the neighbouring country. For that reason, Ethiopia became the first African independent state because two European powers used non-Ethiopian citizens from other African states to liberate Ethiopia (Kevin, 2012).

Two African Kings' Resistance to Colonization

A political comparison of the military achievements between Ethiopian Emperor Haile Selassie and King Akway Cham in Paanywaa shows that each king fought certain European forces as they opposed colonialism in their countries. First, King Akway Cham fought and defeated the British, keeping the Anuak kingdom independent for 15 years (1912-1927). Sadly, his beloved country was annexed to Sudan in 1927 after his death in 1920 (Evan-Pritchard, 1940). According to Kevin (2012), Ethiopia was colonized by the Italians for five years. Kevin stated that Ethiopia was under Italian rule from 1936 until 1941. After Addis Ababa was captured by the Italian forces in May 1936, Emperor Haile Selassie fled to Europe and he lived in exile. His return to his native country was facilitated by the British, who had been supporting Ethiopia and its expansion into Anuak land.

King Akway Cham was an unsung hero in African history! He never ran to a foreign country for his personal security. According to King Akway, it was an insult for the Anuak king to leave his nation for a foreigner to rule it. He remained in Otalo where his forces defeated the British at the battle of Juom in 1912. The distance between Otalo and Juom was less than 30 miles, yet British could not capture it! It proved that King Akway was the bravest African king in the colonial period. For the next fifteen years, the British were blocked from coming to Otalo until the king died (Evans-Pritchard, 1940).

His bravery and anti-colonization agenda kept British out of the Anuak nation. King Akway Cham was the greatest king because he invested in national security. His priority was to protect Anuaks. He provided guns to the Adongolese to defend themselves from foreign aggressors. In 1912, King Akway prepared to meet with British troops and his forces were at a similar level in military capabilities—both forces were armed with rifles. As a result, the battle of Juom not only tested British military power, but it also challenged British superiority in the battlefield (Collins, 1983). When the British conceded defeat, King Akway Cham was the only man in the African continent who had defeated the British.

While he resided in Otalo, the British were unable to reach Otalo and were defeated on the battlefield and were forced to retreat to Akobo town where they were based. During the fight, two British commanders were killed while hundreds of soldiers lay dead on the ground (Evans-Pritchard, 1940). Dhaldiim warriors or freedom fighters admitted that more than 100 British soldiers were found dead when the war ended. Akway Agada confirmed that number: "This figure [of 100] was known because more than 100 guns were captured during the fight." It was a total defeat, which the British cannot deny to this day.

It is astonishing to learn that African history did not acknowledge the great achievements of King Akway Cham who crushed the British army more successfully than Emperor Haile Selassie, who was defeated by the Italian invaders. It took British fifteen years to visit the Adongo region where they were repelled militarily (Evans-Pritchard, 1940). However, when King Akway Cham was alive, there was no room for imperialism in the Anuak kingdom. Kevin (2012) revealed that Emperor Haile Selassie defeated Italian forces in Ethiopia because of British and French military support. According to him, both British and French used other African armies to defeat the Italians from Ethiopia in 1941. Overall, the Anuak people resisted colonialism more effectively than Ethiopians. So, the Anuak's military prowess was felt by the British, who committed many atrocities in Africa.

Both King Akway Cham and Emperor Haile Selassie fought with the European invaders using modern weapons of the time. These two leaders were the first Africans to have firearms and the British could not penetrate Anuak territory. As a result, the Anuak people remained free from British control and injustices. It revealed that Anuaks knew their rights; so, they would not accept being slaves under British control. Furthermore, Anuak political institutions are based on values and principles that rejected any form of slavery or injustice! Any form of slavery or injustice is rejected whether it be imposed on them by foreigners or their own leaders.

Cuai political development, since its inception, enabled Anuaks to live in a free society. For instance, when an Anuak headman abuses his power, his followers move away from him. The leader soon finds himself isolated because of his unfair treatment. His supporters would stop going to Bura (the parliament) as a protest against his poor leadership. In Anuak politics, an unpopular leader can be easily removed from power through Agem, a coup, to replace him (Evans-Pritchard, 1940). All the political process suggest that Anuak people know their political rights. But whenever those rights are violated, they defend them at all costs! That was the reason they fought the bloodiest war against the British who tried to colonize their nation. Anticipating the injustices of the British in African continent, the Anuak fought to maintain their freedom. They hated mistreatment and slavery. In short, the Anuak kingdom could not accept rules from the United Kingdom as they were incompatible with the values of their kingdom.

King Akway played an important role in resisting British colonization in Anuak country. His determination showed that African people would prevail if they were armed with rifles like Europeans. It also proved that the European capacity to control Africa depended on their military capabilities (Kevin, 2012). For instance, it took the Italians two attempts to invade Ethiopia. Emperor Menelik defeated Italian forces at the Battle of Adwa in 1896. This evidence suggested that European powers would not have controlled Africa at all if Africans had similar weaponry as their enemies. Unfortunately, Europeans came to Africa with rifles and machine guns when most nations used spears, arrows and bows. The history of colonialism becomes clear after examining the military capabilities of European countries.

By contrast, the two African kings who armed their forces with firearms before the Europeans came to colonize their nations, did their best with the type of rifles they had. Overall, King Akway Cham and Emperor Haile

Selassie fought to stop imperialism from entering their countries. Their resistance demonstrated that Europeans would not colonize African nations if they had firearms like the Anuak and Ethiopian kingdoms.

9

King Adongo Agada Akway (2001-2011)

Adongo-Wara-Achang inherited the royal throne in March 2001. After his coronation, he spoke with the Canadian Embassy in Addis Ababa, Ethiopia, to commission funds to open primary schools in Pochalla county. The Canadian Embassy was keen to help King Adongo achieve his educational goals for children in Pochalla to secure a brighter future. Through his hard work, he was able to build schools in greater Pochalla. "The Canadian Embassy provided $40,000 and permanent schools were built in Pochalla, Otalo, Ajwara, Nyium, Obuodi and Okadi," King Akway said. These schools are still functioning today in Pochalla county. King Adongo was the first king to tackle the issue of education in the county. As a former teacher, he believed that education was important as it empowered the community! Maintaining knowledge and skills in the Anuak community was the key to prosperity, political freedom, and development. He wanted to eradicate illiteracy in the county. According to Adongo's plan, schools would accept students from Grade 1 through to Grade 8. Due to lack of resources, not all of them opened to Grade 8—only in Pochalla and Otalo did schools open to Grade 7, according to King Akway.

An Educated King

King Adongo graduated from senior secondary School in Malakal in 1979. Following his graduation from high school, he applied for a teaching job in Jonglei. He was accepted and taught in Pochalla intermediate School. In 1982, Adongo became a school director in Pochalla. Two years later, Pochalla was attacked by the Sudanese rebels, SPLA, in 1984, which closed the schools. This prompted Adongo to move to Khartoum to pursue his higher education. He was accepted in one of the universities in Cairo to study engineering. Before he earned his degree, King Adongo discontinued his study in Egypt and attended the University of Juba in Khartoum. While there, he majored in Education, specialising in mathematics. King Adongo opened schools in Pochalla County and some of those students went on to graduate from various universities in Ethiopia and South Sudan. The primary schools he built provided basic education that enabled students to look for further educational opportunities elsewhere. During the ten years of his reign, the literacy rate in Pochalla increased. His Majesty King Adongo is remembered for these educational opportunities that elevate the children in Pochalla County!

'Gurtong' and Peace

The Anuak people developed a peaceful method to address the issue of killings by holding a culprit accountable in their society. 'Gurtong', a legal process, aims to settle conflict between Anuaks and their neighbouring tribes. **Gurtong** is a compound word. **Gur** meaning blunting, **Tong** meaning spear. Before acquisition of firearms in the late 1800s, Anuaks used spears to fight. In this case, sharpening spears suggested warriors were preparing for war, blunting the spears, on the contrary, meant peace. Hence, **Gurtong** is a peacemaking process to bring warring parties to the negotiating table. It can be used between nations, communities, clans, or families. A year after King Adongo's coronation, he dealt with an unprecedented legal matter! In Anuak legal battles, no previous king presided over a murder case caused by a car accident. But it was obvious that serious crimes related to deaths, injuries and disputed divorces were taken to the royal court, or Kal/Poor, for settlement. According to King Akway, a Kenyan driver who worked for Medair—a Swiss based NGO operating in Pochalla county—accidentally killed an Anuak boy.

Gurtong is the peace agreement that settles killing issues and it also reconciles a family of the victim with the offender. It has been applied in the past to resolve tribal wars with the Nuer and the Murle people. Above all, Gurtong is a legal strategy Anuaks use to stop retaliation. "A car belonging to Medair hit the Anuak boy and killed him,' King Akway said. The boy's parents needed to know who was responsible for the death of their child. Although the boy's family were devastated by their loss, they did not take revenge. If the father had wished to take revenge against the Kenyan in retaliation for his son's death, he would have been able to do so easily. However, he used the Anuak legal system to settle the murder case. The parents of the child sued the Kenyan driver who killed their son in the car accident. "A director of Medair in Pochalla admitted that the Anuak boy was killed by one of their drivers inadvertently," King Akway said. It is imperative to understand the meaning of compensation for loss of life: Gurtong reduces the chance of retaliatory killing. It had been used to resolve murder cases in the Anuak community for centuries. When a Medair director heard about Gurtong, he was willing to pay settlement for the Kenyan driver who worked for Mediar. In this case, representatives of the Medair were told to go to Otalo to settle the compensation. This took place in 2002.

The Anuak legal system has worked efficiently for centuries. **Kwor** is a crime that requires compensation for a life lost or disability caused. It is divided into two categories: unintentional killing and premeditated murder. So, compensation, for instance, an accidental killing had a lower price because an offender did not intend to kill the person. Overall, taking a human's life is a crime that is punishable in the Anuak nation. Consequently, the killer is punished for the crime he/she committed.

A compensation structure outlines what needs to be paid for a premeditated murder: five Dimuys, five cows, a string of bells for the drum dance, Teenjeth, a particular type of bead, a gun, traditional spears, and a big bull. The price for unintentional killing is cheaper: four Dimuys, five cows, a string of bells for the drum dance, Teenjeth, a gun, traditional spears, and a big bull. Those are the penalties for taking a human's life intentionally or unintentionally. In addition, a big bull is the meal for both parties after the agreement is reached. At the end of the peace agreement, the bull is killed and divided equally between the two parties. According to Anuak culture, eating the bull together signifies peace and reconciliation for the two families.

The Anuak people believe that there is no price on human life. In fact, life is irreplaceable! Nevertheless, Gurtong is a rational approach to reduce crimes by punishing criminals to compensate for crimes they had committed and discourage revenge attacks. In the example above, the family of the deceased and the representative of Medair signed the Gurtong agreement in Otalo in 2002. To conclude the peaceful process, representatives of the killer started blunting their spear. This suggested acceptance of guilt, cleansing, compensation and seeking of forgiveness. After the admission of guilt, the victim's family also blunted their spear to prove that they would not retaliate. They accepted the compensation while forgiving the killer. This is how the Anuak people solved murder cases in their society effectively and peacefully.

The Gurtong process amazed Westerners who witnessed the agreement for the first time. European and American representatives saw how Gurtong was simple, effective and peaceful. Shortly after the agreement was made in Otalo, Kwachakworo (Dr. Conrad Perner) created a Gurtong website to

address tribal conflicts that led to killing and injury of people in South Sudan. Without a doubt, the Western observers admitted that the Anuak people had the best system to solve serious crimes—more effectively than most South Sudanese tribes.

For the Anuaks, Gurtong has been the legal principles for centuries as it is believed to have begun at the inception of Anuak political system during the period of Cuai. According to Evans-Pritchard, sometimes a murderer must give his son or daughter to the family of the deceased. If he cannot afford the compensation required for settlement, the murderer surrenders himself to the family of the victim. As a rule, he would not be killed. "In the latter case, certain families hand over sleeping mats, some spearheads and Dimuy beads, and the blade of a hunting spear is blunted on a stone and put into the house of the murdered man's family. With these rites having been duly observed, all rancour and desire for revenge on the victim's family ceases," Evans-Pritchard.

King Akway Agada Akway Coronated in 2012

King Akway Agada was crowned on the 25 April 2012. He is the twenty-fourth king of the Anuak kingdom. After his coronation, the new king appointed his royal cabinet to work with him at the Poor/Kal (parliament or Court). Poor and Bura are two distinct political systems that run parallel in the Anuak nation. But this section focuses on kingship (Nyic), which developed from Kwar (headmanship/ chiefdom). Details about Kwar will be discussed in the next chapters. In the Anuak parallel system, Nyic is similar to the presidential system, while Kwar is similar to the parliamentarian system. Nyiya is singular for king while Nyiye is the plural. In this political setting, Nyiya serves for life but Kwaaro (headman or chief) can be removed when he loses majority support. The structure of the Anuak kingship designs key positions for top government officials to run the administration more effectively. The following people are the current government's officials in Otalo (Leela), the capital of the Anuak kingdom. Positions, duties, and roles of each person in the cabinet are listed in the royal structure:

- **Nyiya/Rwoth** (King): Akway Agada Akway is the head of the nation.
- **Nyibur** (Prime Minister): Akway Ojunni. Nyibur stays at the rear of the king's private home. He oversees the king's household. He provides security to the queens. He has a special status that gives him more privilege in the administration. He can walk with his shoes on and can also wear a hat in the palace. It is his duty to make sure the queens do not quarrel among themselves. He also keeps his eye on the followers. Because the king rules in more villages, the king appoints Nyibur to represent him in other villages where he may not be able to attend.
- **Nyikugu** (king's deputy) emblems holder, Attorney General/Chief Justice: Oman Obel. Nyikugu deals with legal cases such as compensation for injuries. He has the power to crown kings. All royal materials and horns used for the coronation are under his authority. It is his responsibility to blow the horn. When the king is not in Otalo, Nyikugu is acting king.
- **Nyithengo** (deputy of Nyikugu): Opara Owity. Nyithengo oversees security in the department called Jaye (security and military advisors) always ensuring the safety of the king.
- **Nyiatuel** (Minister of Interior and Public Relations) in the department called **Cwat**: Okello Oboya Opir. Nyiatuel announces current events. He also receives donations from commoners such as leopard skin, ivory and other valuables people offer to the king. He is responsible for placing feathers on the king's headdress.
- **Nyiatuel** Mar- Bat Boogi (deputy): Chijwok Jok. His duty is to wash the king's cloths. He is also the private secretary. He implements protocols in the palace. Chijwok prepares tea and other soft drinks for the king.
- **Nyikeeno** (food service affairs): Oriee Bah. Senior Nyikeeno does not cook, but he makes sure that there is sufficient beer and flour for kitchen (Ajom) needs.
- **Deputy Nyikeeno** (cook/chef): Agwa Omot Agwa. He prepares food for the king in Ajom and serves it in the front dining room.
- **Kwach Kodo** (drum beater/whistle-blower): Othow Cham. Kwach

Kudo supervises the internal affairs of the queens. Sometimes he prepares food in the court for special occasions. He is responsible for beating drums in case of an emergency but also for the coronation, and for the king's royal dance. The special drum is called **Odol-Kodo**.

- **Mee** (king's maternal uncles): They are stationed closer to the queens' residence to protect Panduong (the house of queens).
- **Katha-Radhi/Kwach-Lwak** (General Chief of Staff): Odwuong Chamchalla Cham. He is the head of Adongolese Royal Army.
- **Deputy Katha Radhi:** Obang Omot Akane. The deputy supports the General Chief of Staff of the royal army.
- **Lwak-Mar-Tiera Atuel** (another military force) in a branch of Atuel: Okach Ojulu. Atuel is always located in the north of Panduong.
- **Lwak-Tiera Atuel** (assistant): Obono Okoth.
- **Lwak-Mar-Kaadi** (military intelligence) responsible for protecting buildings on the southside of Panduong: Odol Owar (Odol Nyatuuk). They protect Dhi-Poor-Oballa (the king's entrance). They assess the

security situation. When there is a plan to attack an enemy, they will go to the enemy's territory and plans the strategy.
- **Okony Okach** (Assistant to Lwak-Mar-Kaadi)
- **Lwak-gan-duong** (special forces) that protects Olaam, the king's private house and conference hall.
- **Lwak-Nga-Apeiya**: all royal guards.
- **Nyipem (prince)**: the uncrowned son of the king. Nyipem leads hunting and fishing expeditions. He oversees villages outside of his father's residency. He escorts his sisters to their husband's homes when they get married.
- **Bimm** (tax collector) currently waiting appointment.

Note: all aspects of the king's daily activities, from security to food preparation are done by men. This has been the protocol since the establishment of the Anuak kingdom. The Anuak developed a monarch system that includes all branches of government. The key positions in the kingdom proves that the Luo were the builders of the Kush kingdom (Onyala, 2019).

Buildings of The Royal Court

A: Panduong: House of the Queens.
B: Apeiya: all buildings in the court.
C: Okuo: house of the senior queens.
D: Poor: palace/court.
E: Olaam: King's bedroom.
F: Ajom: kitchen.
G: Diidek: living/conference room.
H: Thworu: drum post. The drum is used for communication: It is like a radio station/ military signal for the army. In case of emergency/coup, the drum is beaten to inform or warn the public about the events that are about to take place.

10

Headmen and Their Role in The Anuak Nation

An interview with Ochalla Ojulu Ojwato was conducted on 23 March 2019: The theme of the discussion focused on the political role played by the headman of Olaw village in the Rwanye region. He provided insights about the political system in Olaw. Ochalla asserted that the headman was a political leader and a commander-in-chief of the army of the village he lived in. Ochalla is one of the Anuak elders who lives in Brisbane, Australia. He is immensely knowledgeable in Anuak politics and history. He was born in Olaw. When he was a young boy, he learnt from elders who worked at the Bura, or local parliament. Due to his early exposure and education in Anuak politics, he is considered a living library, an excellent historian in Anuak political systems. Ochalla was 60 years old during the interview in 2019.

Kwar (*Headmanship*) and Nyic (*Kingship*)

To understand Anuak political systems, readers need to learn key political terms:

Anuak Language	English
1: Athibil	1: Politics
2: Nyic	2: Kingship/kingdom
3: Kwar	3: Headmanship/chiefdom
4: Bura	4: Parliament
5: Poor/ Kal	5: Palace/court
6: Nyiya/ Rwoth	6: King
7: Kwaaro	7: Headman/chief
8: Bangi	8: Acephalous/stateless nation
9: Gurtong	9: Peace agreement
10: Agem	10: Revolution, coup, rebellion

Opposite words are listed from Anuak to English

> Nyiya/King　　　　　　　Bang/Commoner
> Kwaaro/Headman　　　　Bang/Commoner
> Nyic/Kingdom　　　　　Bangi/Acephalous Society
> Kwar/Headmanship　　　Bangi/Acephalous Society

The word Bang is a singular, while Bangi is the plural. At the same time, Bangi means commoners. In other words, Bangi refers to the people who do not have any political system. Those people live in a stateless nation or acephalous society.

This section concentrates on a theory of Kwar development in Anuak politics. It is the oldest political system that existed in Anuak nation during Cuai rule, the founding father in ancient times. From the onset, the Anuak political institution was developed independently from its rulers. There is a clear definition of the ruler and the political system. Therefore, Anuak political leaders work in the political settings. Furthermore, Cuai was the most influential leader who founded the Kwar system that governed Anuak society. This political institution developed in the time of hunter-gatherer societies (Kevin, 2012). Due to a stable political system, Anuaks were able to live in a social organization that enhanced humanity. In Anuak culture, governing institutions are respected and honoured. Even if someone disagrees with the headman, he still respects the institution. According to Godfrey Lienhardt, Anuak people respect the institution of headmanship everywhere they go in the country. After Cuai built political institutions, he established laws to govern his nation peacefully. As a result of this political structure, Cuai governed an Anuak nation that obeyed rules, promoted egalitarianism, and provided services to the poor. **Kwaaro** is a singular for a headman or chief. While **Kwaari** is the plural of the headmen or chiefs. **Kwar** is the political institution. **Kwaaro** means a rich person! **Cuai** was known for many achievements. Therefore, **Cuai** is also referred to as a creator according to Anuak legend: He invented agriculture and developed a political system that protected Anuak people in the earliest times.

The foundation of the Anuak political system was related to wealth and bravery, according to Ochalla. Since its inception in the ancient world, wealth and bravery were requirements for the candidates who wanted to serve as a headman in the villages. When the political system had grown into a political institution that could run Anuak political affairs, its function was the key reason for political stability in the country. As mentioned above, the rich people who had the resources to provide for the poor people in the community often qualified for political office. "The resources of the headmen at that time were farms, cattle, goats, sheep, Dimuy, and multiple wives," Ochalla said.

Anuak governance is built on rules, humanity, generosity, and egalitarianism. In this political system, the headman is not elected but he inherits the post from his father who served before him. A man from a certain clan is always crowned a headman or chief. The word headman suggests that a man from a ruling clan or a particular family dynasty usually leads. An analysis of the Anuak political system shows that it is clan-based politics. This means it excludes non-clan members from running for political office, but others can be appointed to serve in different positions in the government. "The cohesion of a village is due not only to common residence and common action in war, but also to a common loyalty to a hereditary line of headmen," Evans-Pritchard writes. In this case, transferring power from an incumbent headman to a new ruler is limited to the family members. Often it is brothers, step-brothers, cousins, or uncles, in the ruling clan who are competing for the throne. Since political opportunities are narrowed to some clans, it becomes an inherited post, which is passed down from father to son for generations. Nevertheless, participating in politics requires rules and regulations. To be approved as a candidate for political leadership, the following are behaviours, personalities or marital status that prohibits any candidate from becoming a headman:

> *Greediness or selfishness, cowardice, unmarried, unpatriotic, not coming from the ruling clan.*

On the list for the best candidates invariably includes generosity, bravery, patriotism, coming from the ruling clan and being married. The goal is to make sure the headman is generous and that he would provide social support to the poor in society. The founders of Anuak society believed in humanitarian assistance. For that reason, the headman is committed to serving the community by helping the poor. Sharing or caring for others are key principles which promote egalitarianism in the Anuak nation. Thus, every year after a good harvest, the headman's queens make beer (Kongo) and cook for the supporters in the village.

Keeping Social Harmony

Anuaks are respectful of the institutions that govern the nation! Bura is the parliament where the headman is the head of state. In modern politics, Bura is referred to as a parliamentary system. It develops policies that evaluate the performance of the headmen, hence a vote of no confidence to remove the headman from power is allowed. This article of impeachment or removal is related to the parliamentary system. In Olaw, Pinykwo is the headman's clan that has been ruling the village for generations. Ochalla Banyo was the founder of the Pinykwo lineage, according to Ochalla Ojulu. During the reign of Ochalla Banyo, he fathered two boys, Ojulu-wara-Agut and Okwom-Wara-Agut. In Anuak protocols, kings and headmen are addressed with their mothers' names. Their full official names are Ojulu Ochalla Banyo and Okwom Ochalla Banyo. But it is an honour to address them with their mothers' names. For example, Ojulu-Wara-Agut (means son of Agut). When the Pinykwo dynasty grew larger, the family split into two sections: Ojulu led the bigger section while Okwom led the smaller one.

To understand the Kwar political system better, it is crucial to look at government structure. Below is the example of the government in Olaw run by the Kwaaro or headman. For simplicity, this research looked at the political leader who was in power at Olaw in the 1970s. The structure of the executive office of the headman, Nyigwo Okwom and his cabinet in 1975. The following are the titles, political positions, and individuals' roles in the government:

- **Kwaaro/Rwoth** (Headman or Chief): Nyigwo Okwom, head of the village in Olaw, Rwanye region. He was the political leader and commander-in-chief of the Olaw forces.
- **Nyikugu** (Deputy Headman and Chief Justice): Opothi Ochalla-Wata-Wata. Nyikugu deals with court cases such as compensation for injuries and other legal matters in the community. He assumes leadership when the headman is absent from the village for any duration of time.

- **Nyibur** (Prime Minister): Ojang Winydoori-Wara-Angguu. Nyibur lives near the headman's private home. He provides security to the queens. He has a special status that gives him more privilege in the administration. Nyibur keeps his eye on everyone in Bura. He is the landowner with traditional power to bless the land—he prays for the safety of fishermen and hunters. Nyibur oversees the national healing using power invested in him by membership of the clan that owns a village site. Due to those traditional beliefs, he blesses the army for their services. The Anuak tribe believe that landowners are connected to their ancestral lands and have spiritual power over the land.
- **Nyiatuel** (Minister of Foreign Affairs and Interior): Obuthi Ogurajak. He arranges meetings with visitors who want to meet the headman. He also connects his village with other regions outside of their territory. Nyiatuel plays a key role in the security sector. He leads a military assessment in preparation of attacks. When he returns from the enemy territory, he briefs the headman. Nyiatuel also announces current events. In addition, he receives donations from commoners (Bangi) such as leopard skin, ivory and other valuable things that people give to the headman.
- **Kwach-Lwak/Ketha-Radhi** (General Chief of staff): Nyikew Awel- He is the head of armed forces and commands all military activities.
- **Kare Wang** (security advisor to the headman): Ojulu Nyigwo Akerbell. He reports security concerns directly to Nyikugu. In this case, Ojulu works closely with the deputy headman.
- **Nyibaatbogo** (social secretary and servant for the headman): Gillo Ojuu.
- **Nyikeeno** (food coordinator): Ochalla Agal Chambatha ensures that there is sufficient food and drink available for kitchen (Amoa) services.
- **Nyikeeno Mana Tedo** (cook/chef). Male youths are trained to cook for the headman. They are responsible for preparing stew such as meat, fish, vegetables, or soups. They rotate cooking: Each person is scheduled to cook at different times. Meanwhile, the queens only cook flour or make thick porridge (Kwon) to be eaten with the soup.

Buildings in Bura:

- Panduong: House of the Queens
- Amoa: Kitchen
- Bura: Parliament
- Thworu: Drum post. The drum is used for communication: It is like radio station/or military signal for the army. In case of emergency/coup, drum is beaten to inform public about what happen.

There is another important branch of administrators that play a significant role in the security matters and better governance. "They are called Jaye: a group of retired administrators who can be called to the Bura to assist the headman when they are needed for urgent political issues or deliberation," Ochalla said. They are experienced advisors! They would hold a private meeting with the leadership, deputy, and Minister for Foreign Affairs at a hall conference (Odhiang). Ochalla asserts that all government confidential meetings take place at Odhiang. The following are the names of Jaye, political advisors, at Bura in Olaw parliament in 1975:

- Ongier Tago
- Ogeia Ojulu
- Obuthi-Gurajak
- Ochalla Wata-Wata
- Okach Meet
- Nyigwo Akarabel
- Akwor Ajimthe
- Ochalla Abulle
- Ojulu Gillo
- Okello Aballa
- Aballa Owil

These people advised the headman in political matters and security concerns and have political power to approve, modify or reject the agenda of the headman. People in the Jaye department oversee the checks and balances of the

Anuak political system. After their unanimous decision, they would authorise the headman to implement his political agendas.

The Importance of The Coronation

It is the official inauguration that recognises new leadership. As discussed above, candidates for the headmanship need to show they possess the right values and personality for effective leadership. Consequently, the best candidates for the headmanship are expected to show patriotism, generosity, bravery, intelligence, be married, must come from the ruling clan and must not practice nepotism or favouritism.

On the other hand, there are guidelines that disqualify potential candidates: greediness or selfishness, cowardice, unmarried, unpatriotic, practices nepotism or favouritism and is not from the ruling family.

There is no term-limit for the headman, but he can be removed if he abuses his power. Due to these settings, the duration of the headman in the office depends on his policies and adherence to the rules of law that have governed Bura for thousands of years.

The Impeachment Process

According to Ochalla, the impeachment of the headman from office is based on evidence of abuse of power. Any leader who abuses his power will not last in the office. This occurs, for example, if the headman seeks to punish his political opponents. His political tactic is viewed as intimidating those who disagree with him at Bura on certain political issues. Perhaps, the headman may fine them without good reason. Second, Ochalla states that the headman is prohibited from punishing anyone who did not co-operate with him. This behaviour is intolerable in the Kwar political system and an investigation would be conducted into the headman's actions immediately. If the investigation confirms wrongdoing, the headman loses legitimacy to govern: These are some examples of breaches that could lead to impeachment:
- Headman targets people he does not get along with for punishment.
- Headman brings charges against individuals who disagreed with him

at Bura. For example, bringing charges against someone to pay a cow, goat, sheep, or Dimuy is corruption in Anuak society.
- Headman secretly visits people's homes without informing them in advance. In Anuak governing institutions, the headman and king are forbidden from visiting anyone in their private homes. Instead, friends and relatives can visit these leaders in their residency. The headman of Olaw began inappropriately visiting people's homes. To make matters worse, when the person did not stand up because he did not expect to see him, the headman complained that he was not respected. These allegations are unfounded because every Anuak respects the institution of headmanship including ex-headman (Lienhardt, 1957). According to him, it is the institution that Anuaks respect not necessarily the individual leaders. These allegations are threatening in nature that cannot be tolerated in a democratic society.

Several steps can be taken to resolve political conflicts. Any dictatorship/despotism in Anuak politics can be dealt with according to the rules. There were nine clan members investigating the headman who abused his power. "These nine clans in Olaw had the power to investigate and decide whether the headman could be removed or continue his leadership," Ochalla stated. Hence, the members of those clans studied the reports carefully and gathered more evidence. They analysed the evidence before making any decision for the removal of the headman. When evidence built up, those investigators developed a resolution to the conflict. First, they wanted to ensure that they had reliable sources, which were irrefutable in the court of law. The clans below were responsible for the impeachment of the headman at Olaw in Rwanye.

Dhe Oto: (Family of or clan):
- Ongier War-Tago
- Ogeia Oboya Alual
- Aballa Winyidieri
- Ojang Winyidieri
- Oman Ogaa
- Obuthi Ogurajak

- Okach Meet
- Owil Opiew
- Aballa Okello.

After a thorough investigation, these clans' members met to decide whether the headman had lost his legitimacy to govern. They wanted to know how many people from the clans favoured the removal of the headman. A consensus was required to act against a dictator. During their closed-door meeting, they looked at the majority votes as the best way to resolve the political problem. Hence, the impeachment motion succeeded only when it received more votes. "However, if the majority had voted against the impeachment, the removal process would have to stop immediately because it would be considered (Agem), revolution or coup against the current headman," said Ochalla.

The structure of village headmanship is linked with the clan lineage, which allows sons of the previous headmen to rule their village (Evans-Pritchard, 1940, P.38). In this case, Evans-Pritchard stated that: "the system of village headmanship is based on the lineage structure of the village and both hold it together." While nine clans were responsible for the removal of the headman, another two clans were tasked to perform a coronation of a new leader in Olaw. The clans led by Owil-War-Opiew and Okach-War-Meet were responsible for crowning the new headman. Usually, when concerned members agree to change the leadership, they work to bring another headman to the office. If the meeting agrees to impeach the leader because of his threatening behaviour by imposing unwarranted punishment on innocent people, the members of the two clans begin to look at the backgrounds of the other sons of the previous headmen in Olaw, searching for the right candidate to bring to the office. When they find the right candidate, they fetch him from his maternal uncle's home village to replace the sitting headman. It is imperative that they are meticulously in the steps they take for a smooth transition before the removal of the headman. Ochalla explained that they would secretly bring the approved candidate to Olaw and prepare a military response in case of resistance by the existing headman. They split into two groups! The first group is stationed outside the headman's private home, while another group is sent to his house to ask the headman to leave the room. "At the same time, warning him not to carry any weapons: guns, knives, or spears," said Ochalla. After the headman comes out, he is then arrested. Drums would start beating, declaring the removal of the headman! Evans-Pritchard (1940) wrote that, "In a village revolution, one of the first objects of the party of the aspiration to office is to obtain possession of the drums, which are then beaten to inform the village of the success of the revolution."

Legitimising a New Ruler

It is the rule to prepare a successor before a headman is removed from office. "The first step taken to legitimise the new headman is to place a special bead called Tin-Jo-Olaw or bead of the Olaw people," Ochalla said. According to him, this type of bead is worn by a legitimate leader and it also legitimises his leadership to govern the Olaw people. Through coronation, the successor is officially accepted to rule! "The next step is to take the oath of office the same night while he is wearing the bead and beating Odola, a small drum designed for a crowned headman," Ochalla added. A year later, the big coronation will take place in Olaw. All villages near Olaw will be invited to attend the ceremony.

Following his inauguration, the new leadership assumed responsibility at Bura where the headman and his top officials deliberated and made important decisions on social, political, and military affairs. After the headman in Olaw was crowned, he called on youth groups for a special event, according to Ochalla. During the meeting with these youth groups, his deputy (Nyikugu) performed a traditional blessing in which he put hair of the giraffe's tail (win) in the oil and gently sprayed it on the youths. This is a traditional blessing for safety and health for the new generation; it took place at Weebur-Lero village in Olaw, Ochalla said.

It was the biggest celebration conducted by Nyikugu. This traditional event followed very strict rules. For those who were not present to be sprayed with the oil were assigned to fetch water for their colleagues or age mates, who attended the ceremony with Nyikugu. Ochalla said it was a form of punishment for people who missed the occasion. Therefore, they were warned not to wear shirts throughout the celebration. They could drink beer (Kongo) with their colleagues, but they were not permitted to wear shirts until the end of the celebration. Failing to follow these rules had severe consequences!

As an honour for their obedience, all the youths who attended the traditional blessing ceremony were assigned a girl between the ages of fifteen and eighteen to serve drinks for them. Almost all the girls in the village that age, served the young men on this occasion. Some young men stayed at Bura and their families prepared foods for them. In this case, each man reported what his family cooked to **Nyikugu**, the master of ceremony. When it was time for dinner or lunch, he supervised foods and drinks, determining how many people would go to another's house for dinner. Nyikugu had the power to decide if there were enough food and drinks for a certain number of people. Those youths who were staying in Bura went to their homes at nights while spending the day in Bura residence.

Having proper arrangements in place is very important in Anuak culture and politics. Preparations must be made ahead of time to allow people from different villages to attend the coronation. Kongo (beer) is a popular drink during events such as weddings and social gatherings. It is common for wives of the headman to make kongo, and the headman would invite residents of the village to come and drink at Bura residency. But for this particular event, it was the responsibility for the women whose husbands were staying at Bura to make the beer and report it to their husbands who in turn reported it to Nyikugu. Once the kongo was ready, proper arrangements would be put in place to share the beer. Again, the same rule for sharing food applies to beer. Although they all stay at Bura for the day, the Nyikugu would equally distribute the people in different houses for food and drinks. Nevertheless, before determining how many people would be distributed to the different houses, all foods and drinks would be reported to Nyikugu. Based on the amount of food and beer available, the government officials would facilitate the distribution and services of refreshments fairly and equally to all.

It is understood that missing an important event that all youths were expected to participate in, held severe consequences. The headmen expected that these guidelines would be followed as it is important to educate the future generation about all aspects of manhood and responsibilities. Furthermore, the youths were also expected to attend meetings with the headman. But those who did make it to the meeting could face punishment. Ochalla reported "those who were not present when Nyikugu sprayed oil on young men, or came later from their villages, were ordered to cross the border without wearing their shirts." Some of those people agreed to cross the border without wearing their shirts until they arrived inside their village territory. Meanwhile, those who refused to do so, could be fined for the violation. "Usually, the person paid a cow, bull or money for the violation," Ochalla said.

Naming of an Age Group (Lwak)

Anuak traditional forces are named according to age groups, which are treated like ranks in a military battalion or division. When young men are given a military name, they are ready to defend the nation, hence this is a military graduation. According to Ochalla, the newly named forces could be ordered to attack foreign aggression. This experience on the battlefield would encourage them to protect their nation. This new young generation takes responsibility for security and protection. To honour their service, a celebration of their military success is held at the Bura residency.

Ochalla provided details about what happened in 1975, a few months after Nyigwo Okwom became a headman in Olaw. The headman named his first Lwak as soon as he assumed office. He named the new battalion in Olaw, **Ngach Ngo**. With the headman's approval, Ngach Ngo people were recognised, accepted, and respected by other villages as well as everyone in the Rwanye region and neighbouring states.

Jiy Abut Nam means people are fasting in Anuak language. "The Ngach Ngo people were fasting and could not drink milk or eat meat for a month," said Ochalla. They avoided meat and milk until they killed one of the dangerous animals. Fasting comes to an end after the four weeks when a lion, buffalo, leopard or elephant is killed. Eventually, fasting time was over for the Ngach Ngo after they killed an elephant. They gave ivory to the headman, while they used the hair of the elephant's tail to put beads on. According to Ochalla, it was believed that killing brave animals showed their bravery on the battlefield and it was an opportunity for the youths to acknowledge their responsibility as they progress to manhood. It is crucial to show bravery and readiness to fight against attackers to maintain security in the country. After their return from hunting, people slaughtered cows, goats and sheep for the Ngach Ngo people. At the same time, kongo, or beer, was prepared for them. Their victory is always the biggest celebration in the village.

Headmen of The Pinykwo Dynasty in Olaw

When Ojulu Ochalla was the headman in Olaw, his family continued to rule the village: Kur Ojulu, Othow Ojulu, Didiumo Ojulu, and Ochan Ojulu. Okwom Ochalla's family ruled Olaw. In the first term, Okwom was removed from the office. But later he was reinstated as the headman in Olaw. Okwom was the longest-serving headman in the history of Olaw, according to Ochalla. During his first and second terms, Okwom was removed from power due to false accusations made against him by his political rivals. However, when his successors failed to meet expectations of the villagers, Okwom was recalled to lead his people once again. After he died, his son, Nyigwo Okwom was crowned the headman in Olaw. While the Anuak culture embraces a diverse group of clans, which brings landowners and immigrants from other villages or regions together, the political power is restricted to only the ruling clan. In this region, it is restricted to Pinykwo Dynasty in Olaw.

11

The Kwar Political System in Itang

An interview with Obang Okumu Okom was conducted on 27 April 2019: The discussion concentrated on the origin of the political system in Itang and Ray Gillo military achievements in the nineteenth century. Obang lived in Minneapolis, Minnesota, at the time of the interview.

A headman provides leadership that unites all the villages he rules. Evans-Pritchard (p. 38) states that: "A headman gives a village a sense of unity and provides leadership and encourages co-operation. He symbolises the solidarity of the village and its political exclusiveness," he said. The political system that ruled Itang for centuries traces its origins to Cuai, the founder of Anuak political system (Pritchard, 1940). People who settled in Itang were direct descendants of Cuai. The establishment of Cuai political dynasty in the Openo region was initiated by King Gillo Ochudho, the first king in the Anuak kingdom. King Gillo took power from his grandfather-Cuai after he died, according to Anuak legend.

Kwar and **Nyic** political systems all originated from one source—Cuai! Obang said that when Cuai was a headman, his older son committed adultery with one of his younger wives. "As a result, Cuai ordered his armed men to capture him, but during the arrest, the adulterer was killed," he said. Cuai ordered his men to stab him, but he did not mean to kill him. He meant to take his cattle and let him suffer from hunger. Due to the misunderstanding, his son was killed for committing adultery. When those men came back and reported that his son was killed, Cuai was devastated.

Cuai's grief led him to ordering his bodyguards to execute the person who killed his son. This suggested that one of the men who was ordered by Cuai to kill his son for committing adultery had to be killed too. The reaction from the village community was negative and they blamed Cuai for abusing his power. They said the man followed his orders and he was innocent. This was the beginning of chaos in the Cuai Dynasty for years to come. Due to the sudden deaths of the two men in the community, Cuai's popularity diminished. This political crisis created lawlessness in the village where Cuai ruled, Obang said. The revenge killing prompted the people to lose their trust in his leadership and legitimacy to govern. "As a result, the nation was in anarchy. To make matters worse, Cuai stayed in the house and did not come out to resolve any social and political problems," he revealed.

During that time, there was no effective leadership in the nation. Consequently, when a person raised an issue of stealing or claims of adultery, Cuai would tell the plaintiff to go and retaliate. Again, this approach encouraged the plaintiffs to commit adultery with the wife of the adulterer, or the man would take sexual revenge against another man's wife. Similarly, when somebody was killed by accident, Cuai encouraged the family of the deceased to avenge the death of their daughter or son. The cycle of retaliation killed a lot of people! A solution was urgently needed to resolve anarchy in the nation where Cuai was leader. "It was Cuai's young grandson Gillo who advised his grandfather to stop the retaliation methods among people in the community," Obang said.

The Rise of a Young Leader

While Gillo was a young boy living with his grandfather, he realised that Cuai lacked proper strategies to resolve social and political issues in the nation. With courage and care for his grandfather's success, Gillo suggested some effective approaches to resolve the problems of adultery, killing and stealing in Anuak society. Gillo suggested that instead of retaliation, it would be better to fine the man who committed adultery. This meant compensation for the injured or the aggrieved was required. If a death occurred, the family of the deceased would also be compensated. Gillo also recommended to his grandfather, that if property was stolen, it must be returned to the rightful owners. Cuai was impressed while he listened to Gillo's advice! Eventually, he sent Gillo to Bura, the parliament where lawmakers worked to restore law and order, according to Obang. Here Gillo learned leadership skills. He was involved in the daily politics at Bura, which would prepare him to lead the nation.

Examining the political trends at that time, it indicated that Cuai was getting older and his health was deteriorating. He was preparing Gillo as his successor before he died. "Gillo restored law and order when Cuai passed away because he gave power to his grandson," Obang said. Cuai faced the dilemma of ending headmanship, the political institution that he built from scratch. The rules of Cuai would have been perfect if he had many sons to replace him after he died. Unfortunately, his older son was killed, and his remaining son was too young to rule the nation. Facing this dilemma, Cuai appointed his grandson, Gillo to carry his legacy to the next generation. As the founder of the Kwar political system, he bent the rules to promote Gillo to the leadership and in doing so saved Cuai political institutions.

Interestingly, this political understanding between Gillo and his grandfather, who trusted him to lead the nation, was not accepted by everyone in the family. When the son of Cuai became older, he did not accept his father's decision to give the throne to Gillo, Obang revealed. As a result, a power struggle for succession began. After Gillo took power, Cuai's son, Othwon, claimed that the headmanship belonged to Cuai lineage; Othwon wanted to take power from Gillo! Although Gillo's mother, Koori, was a daughter of Cuai, Gillo himself belonged to another clan. Therefore, he could not be the heir to the throne of Cuai, according to the rules. Political opportunity opens to people of certain clans or families but not everyone—traditionally it is given to the sons of former headmen who are members of that family only. More importantly, eligibility for headmanship required a candidate to be a son of the crowned headman. This requirement disqualified Gillo because his father was not crowned. A peculiarity in the Cuai political system insisted that every candidate for headman be a son of the former headman who served in the office before (Evans-Pritchard, 1940). This mandatory policy restricted legitimacy and eligibility to only a few people. For that reason, the children of Cuai wanted Gillo to resign. "When Cuai's family demanded Gillo to step down from leadership, Gillo refused and continued to rule," Obang stated.

Two Political Systems in One Nation-State

Due to Gillo's refusal to hand political power to Othwon, the younger son of Cuai, he changed **Bura** into **Poor**, which created two distinct political systems in Anuak politics, Obang explained. Evans-Pritchard (p. 38) wrote: "There are two distinct political systems, that of nobles (kings) which is found in the east and south-east and that of the village headmen (Kwaari plural, Kwaaro singular) which is found in the rest of the country."

Gillo structured his political system known as Nyic (**kingship**). To make it different from Kwar (**headmanship/chiefdom**), he used materials his father brought from the river as requirements for crowning the king. Those royal emblems used in the coronation of kings were unique. The kingship adopted most of the policies of Cuai, which required only sons of the former king to be crowned. This change in the Anuak political structure created two parallel systems. Hence, the kingship's house or parliament is called **Poor/Kal**. On the other hand, **Bura** remained for the Cuai Political Dynasty and headmen in general. Due to political changes, Gillo kept Poor for the kingdom. The word, **Cuai** means creator in the Luo language. This showed that Cuai was not just a man, but he was the founder of the Anuak political systems. Therefore, people from his clan are called people of Cuai (Watcuaia or Jowatcuaia). The Kwar political system is thousands of years old, while Nyic has established 500 years ago.

Gillo formed a new political system intentionally to move away from the Cuai Dynasty. He planted seeds for the new political institution that became more powerful in the 1880s. In addition, Gillo changed his title from **Kwaaro** to **Nyiya**. But official titles for the leaders in the two political systems remain the same. For example, an official title for both king and headman is **Rwoth**. It is overlapped or used interchangeably. This is how Gillo Ochudho aligned the two political systems in the Anuak nation.

To implement the two political systems in one country, Gillo relocated Othwon to another region far away from Adongo. King Gillo moved his uncle further away from him to continue the Cuai political system. King Gillo organised a big force to travel with Othwon as he searched for a new location for his political headquarters. Unfortunately, during their long journey from Adongo to Openo, Othwon died of natural causes, according to Obang. But his son, Gweno Othwon, arrived safely with the group at their destination in Itang, Openo state. Immediately, the Cuai family settled in Itang and re-established the Cuai political system in Openo. "After their settlement in Itang, Gweno became the first headman of Itang," Obang stated. According to him, Gweno Othwon showed leadership skills and responsibility before their arrival in Itang. For that reason, the king's delegation and members of Cuai's family appointed him as first Kwaaro in Itang after their arrival to save the Cuai Dynasty from disappearing.

From this time, Bura changed its rules to allow Bura to find a successor who was a grandson of the headman to rule when people reached deadlock for successor. The amendment of Cuai's rules removed restrictions and made it possible for grandchildren from the Cuai Dynasty to qualify for headmanship. According to the old rules, it was illegal for both Gillo and Gweno to be the headmen because their fathers were not crowned. This was a natural selection process to reduce the number of candidates in Nyic and Kwar alike. Evans-Pritchard (p. 48) asserted that a man can be appointed a headman only if his father once held the position. Hence, people who lost legitimacy to govern formed another section of the ruling clan called **Tung Dwong**. Similarly, those who lost nobility in kingship are called **Jowatong**. To understand local politics in Itang, below is a list of the headmen who ruled for centuries.

In the origin of Anuak political system, Cuai was the founder and his grandchildren continued to rule.

Othwon Cuai, Headman

1: Gweno Othwon Cuai was the first headman in Itang in Openo state.
2: Akalejay
3: Gillo
4: Ray

Itang's Acquisition of Firearms

Rwoth Ray-War-Gillo was responsible for securing Itang's territory and the Anuak nation. "While Gweno was a headman in Itang, he sired a son called Akalejay. When he died, Akalejay became the headman of Itang, and he had a son named Gillo. After Gillo became a headman, he Fathered Ray, Ojaa, Okom and Gugo. When Gillo passed away, he wanted Ray to take leadership," Obang said. Ray Gillo became a leader in Itang as it was acquiring firearms from Ethiopia. Ray Gillo bought firearms for the nation's self-defence and his military achievements are famous in Anuak history. Ray was the best leader of his generation who defended his people from foreign aggressors. He stood up for the Anuak people in war and peace, fighting to protect the rights of the Anuak people to live in a free nation and not controlled by foreigners.

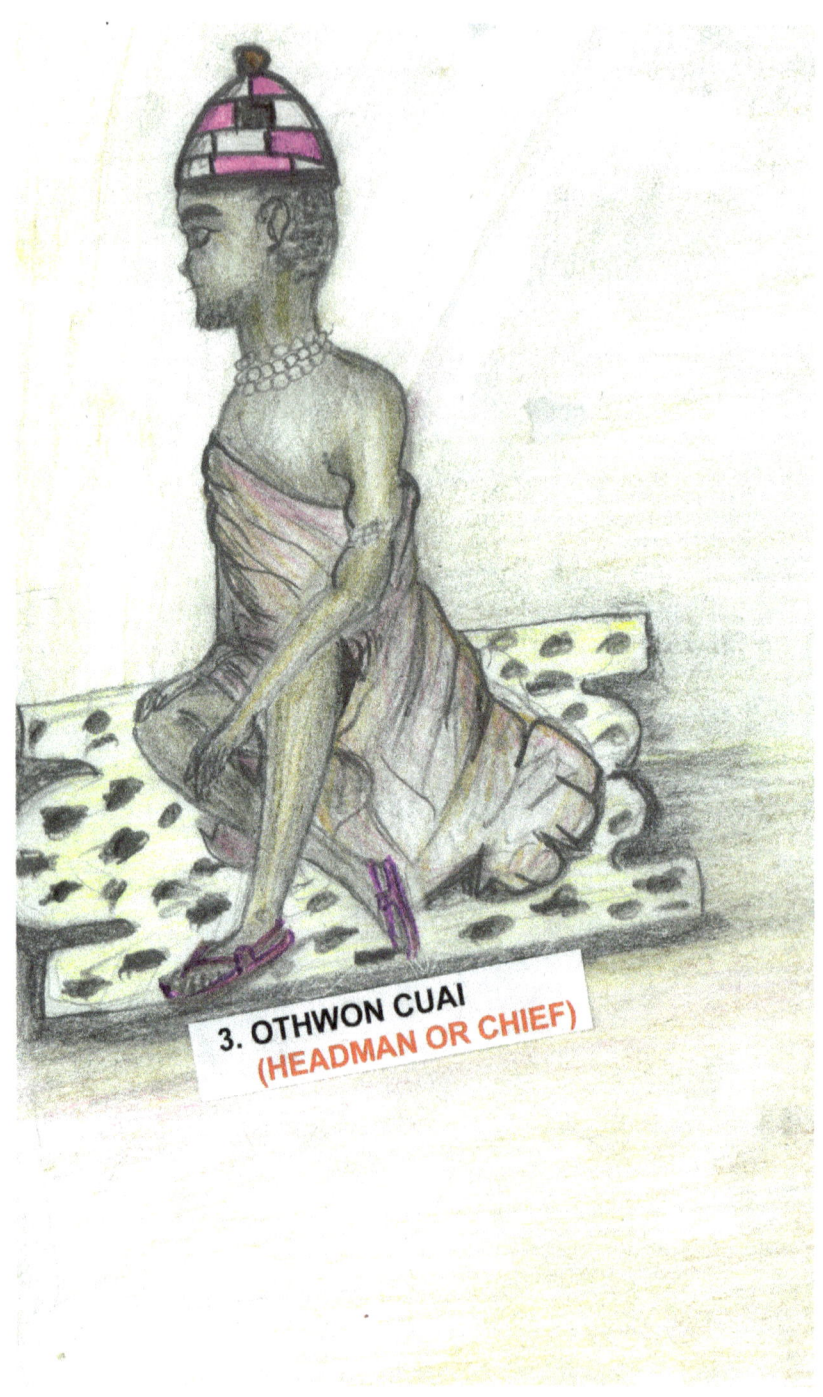

3. OTHWON CUAI (HEADMAN OR CHIEF)

Obang said before his coronation, Anuak people in Itang were unaware of the Opo tribe. Their existence was discovered when some Anuak hunters encountered Opo out hunting. "Anuaks attacked them and brought war captives to Itang after defeating Opo people in the fight." he said. The attack of the Opo people was part of a wider plan to keep foreigners out of Anuak land. It was border protection. The Anuaks' rules for combat prohibited killing prisoners of war, mostly children and women. Those rules were established thousands of years ago during Cuai rule in the ancient times. Obang explained that "some of the captured Opo people went back to Opo land, but others remained in the Anuak land permanently."

After the coronation of Ray Gillo as the headman in Itang, he studied the borderland with Opo people. His administration found that Opo people were neighbours. They lived near Itang, but neither tribe knew each other. The earlier reason for the attack was because the Anuak hunters believed that the Opo people were intruders. Now, Anuak people knew where the Opo people lived. To prevent future land disputes with them, Ray demarcated the boundary between the Openo region and its neighbouring tribes. Above all, he was the architect for demarcating the border with the Opo tribe. He also demarcated the Anuak-Oromo border using a mountain that separated the two nations: It is called **Kewa-Kidi**, which means our natural border is the mountain (Ethiopian escarpment in English). In other words, **Kew** means border, while **Kidi** is the maintain. The reason for demarcating borders was to monitor foreigners who tried to enter Anuak country illegally. Anuaks loved to live in peace and they wanted peace with their neighbours. To maintain peace and friendly relations, Ray opened a market between Anuak and Opo people so that both communities were able to trade with each other peacefully, Obang said.

Ethiopians Attempted Invasion of Gambella

The agreement signed by Anglo-Egyptian Sudan and the Ethiopian kingdom in 1902 brought Ethiopian forces into Anuak land, according to Collins. This was the beginning of the Ethiopians' invasion of Anuak country. It should be made clear that the British made an agreement with the Ethiopian Emperor Menelik to destroy the Anuak people. As a result, Itang ruler Ray Gillo fought against Ethiopian forces, during the 1900s. "After the 1902 agreement was signed, the port in Itang was transferred from Itang to Gambella town. However, before it was transferred, Ray Gillo was allied to the British authority in Gambella," he said. When the port was in the vicinity of Itang, there was mutual interest between Ray Gillo and the British. In their agreements, Obang said British gave guns to the headman of Itang, and Ray Gillo provided leopard skins and ivory to the British in return. At that time, selling ivory and leopard skins was a lucrative business for the Anuak people to arm themselves with rifles or guns. According to their agreements, Ray Gillo was to send tusks and leopard skins to the British authority in Gambella town. "Ray Gillo sent his people to Gambella but before reaching Gambella town, his delegation was arrested by Ethiopian military," Obang said.

Ray's delegation was held prisoner at the Koi military base. When Ray received a report from his people in the prison, he negotiated their release through co-operation with another leader in Pinykew, Rwoth Ojulu Obulu (Kwaaro-War-Obulu). However, Ojulu's attempt to secure their release was unsuccessful and reported to Ray's administration that the Ethiopian authorities refused to release the people detained illegally. In Anuak politics, each leader is in control of his territory. Hence, to pass through Ojulu Obulu's territory, Ray Gillo needed permission from him, according to Obang! "Ray respected War-Obulu's authority in his territory and asked him to give him sixty personnel to show the way for his 300-armed men," he said. Finally, Ojulu Obulu gave permission to Ray's forces to cross into Pinykew land.

Ray Gillo was the most powerful leader in the Openo region and the second powerful man in the nation, behind King Akway Cham, who defeated the British. Ray ordered his armed forces to confront the Ethiopians holding Anuak people unlawfully. Obang stated: "Ray's forces arrived at night and surrounded the military barrack in which Anuak prisoners were kept. In the early morning, while the Ethiopians were raising flag, Obono, a chief of staff of Itang forces, walked straight to one of the Ethiopian officers and stabbed him in the neck, killing him instantly." Immediately, Anuak forces opened fire and the Ethiopian forces were defeated. The Ethiopian forces could not resist the disciplined and well-organised forces of Itang. After the Ethiopians were defeated, Ray's forces were able to free their fellow Anuaks. The attack on Koi garrison was the first military confrontation between the Anuaks and Ethiopians. The operation aimed to release the Anuak people wrongly arrested. This marked the beginning of a continuing war with the Ethiopian army each time they came to Itang. Following the defeat of Ethiopian army at Koi, they left the area permanently.

Anuaks Refuse to Pay Tax to a Foreign Government

Ethiopian troops second attempt to enter Anuak land was to collect taxes from them. According to Collins, in 1916, Majid Abud, an Ethiopian officer was sent to punish the Anuak people in Openo who refused to pay taxes to the Ethiopian kingdom. The Majid expedition to Gambella was another attempt by the Ethiopian authority to exert its power in the Anuak nation. The tax collecting mission was under the agreement of 1902 between the Ethiopian government and Anglo-Egyptian Sudan (Collins, 1983). Despite the Ethiopian army's defeat at Koi, Majid accepted his assignment from Gore authority: He was going to suppress any Anuak who refused to recognise Ethiopian sovereignty in Gambella. "Majid proved loyal to the emperor and on his orders led an Ethiopian punitive expedition into the Baro salient in 1916 to punish those Anuaks who had refused to recognise Ethiopian sovereignty and to wage guerrilla warfare across the frontier in Sudan," Collins said.

Unsurprisingly, the Anuak people refused to pay taxes to the Ethiopian government because they argued they were not Ethiopian citizens, nor did they live in Ethiopia. Anuaks were not subjects of Emperor Menelik! The Anuak people lived in their own country. Therefore, the Ethiopians' invasion of Gambella was unacceptable to them. Everyone in Itang including Ray Gillo, who was headman at the time, rejected the invasion in Gambella in the Openo region. As leader of an independent Openo region he would not allow Ethiopians to come from the highlands, miles away, to impose taxes on them in Itang. In Anuak politics, no leader imposed his /her will on people who lived in other villages not under his jurisdiction or authority. Thus, Ray Gillo rejected the Ethiopians' plan to collect taxes from the Anuak people in Itang and beyond.

In the Anuak federation, every leader was independent in his place, but there was co-operation with other leaders in different states regarding national security. The very principles of the Anuak governing institutions were violated by the Ethiopian authorities when it imposed taxation on the people of Itang. The Anuaks' refusal to pay these taxes resulted in a bloody war with the Ethiopian forces, according to Collins. Blocking Ethiopian people from entering Gambella demonstrated that Anuaks had never been part of the Ethiopian kingdom prior to the agreement that divided them into two countries (Collins, 1983). Fighting broke out between Anuaks and Ethiopian invading forces that were violating their inalienable rights as natives of the land.

Defending national sovereignty is a responsibility of all leaders in the country. Therefore, Anuak people had the right to defend themselves from Ethiopians' aggression. Following their first defeat, the Ethiopian army was well prepared and in larger numbers. They were able to defeat Anuak people after a bloody war that took many lives from both sides (Collins, 1983). "[Majid and the Ethiopians forces] defeated the Anuaks in a bloody engagement in Itang on the Baro River but had to withdraw before carrying out any hostilities in Sudan," Collins stated. This deadly attack was a retaliation for the defeat at Koi. When the fighting ended, the Ethiopian army did not stay near Itang due to fear of being attacked again. As a result, the Ethiopian army withdrew from the area returning to Gore where they came from (Collins, 1983). It did not stop Anuak people's determination to resist Ethiopian rule every time they came to Gambella in the Openo region. Overall, Anuak people defended their freedom when those inalienable rights were violated by foreigners.

Independence Defended

Following the evacuation of Ethiopian forces from the vicinity of Itang, Ray Gillo took military action against the Murle tribe in Southern Sudan. The Murle people were notorious for cattle rustling, child-abduction and raiding villages in Anuak land. Under the leadership of Ray, the people of Itang launched a counterattack to stop the Murle from their criminal activities (Collins,1983). Since the introduction of firearms to the Anuak nation, each leader from his region vowed to deal with any foreign aggression or intruders in their land. During Ray's leadership and his contemporary leaders, they did not recognise that their beloved country was divided. They still believed they lived in their nation-state. For their collective defence, Anuak leaders agreed to protect and defend their land from all invaders. Collins (1983) asserted that in 1932, Anuak people from the Openo region crossed the Akobo river and they were joined by their fellow Anuaks from Southern Sudan to attack the Murle. During the fight, Anuaks killed Murle men and captured eighty people, mostly women and children; they also seized hundreds of cattle (Collins, 1983, p. 376). As a result of attacking the Murle, the British administration demanded that the Ethiopian government return captured Murle and their cattle to the colonial government in Sudan.

British diplomats pressured the Ethiopian government in Addis Ababa to act against the Anuaks who attacked the Murle. In 1932, Ethiopian Emperor Haile Selassie appointed Majid Abud as the Ethiopian frontier agent to confront Anuak's villages. This was 16 years after the Ethiopian attack on Gambella (Collins, 1983). Majid came with a new order from the Ethiopian authority to collect Murle captives and cattle. The order was to return them to Sudan. In February 1933, Majid and his forces arrived in Baat Gillo state with 360 Ethiopian soldiers. Colonial authorities patrolled the Akobo border to stop Ethiopian Anuaks from entering the Sudan side, according to Collins.

To obtain the release of the Murle, Ethiopian troops did not use force. Instead, they used diplomacy with the headmen in Baat Gillo region. The Ethiopian army negotiated with the Anuak leaders for the release of the Murle women and children who were captured during the attack. Due to their non-violent approach, Ethiopians were able to collect some of the captives and cattle. Ethiopian troops took those Murles to Akobo in Sudan (Collins,1983). Since 1902, the British had been pushing Ethiopians to enter Anuak land where they had never been before. Through decades of Anuak resistance, Ethiopians admitted that their kingdom never reached Gambella. Yet, they were pushed to invade it. This came after Emperor Menelik and Anglo-Egyptian Sudan made the agreement to ruin the Anuak independent state and divide their land (Collins 1983). Their common goal was to destroy Anuak's power and subdue them in both countries—Ethiopia and Sudan. Ethiopian troops took the captured Murles and gave them to British Commissioner Tunnicliffe in

Akobo town, and they returned to Gambella, Ethiopia. According to Collins, Ethiopians travelled through Jokaw in Southern Sudan to reach Gambella.

Majid Abud Claimed Nuer Pastoralists to be Ethiopians

Collins (1983) stated that on their way back to Ethiopia, between Dikony and Openo rivers in the Bur-Obey area, Majid claimed a small section of Jikany Nuer, people who grazed their cattle inside Anuak's territory in Ethiopia. This was the first time Ethiopians had penetrated deep into Anuak land! Nuers came to Anuak land in the dry season, but they never lived in those villages. It is a common tradition for pastoralists to move with their cattle from one place to another looking for green pastures. Due to ignorance, Majid Abud announced his discovery of Nuer people to be subjects of Emperor Haile Selassie, according to Collins. Immediately, he wanted to collect taxes from them as a sign of their submission and confirmation of the Nuers' allegiance to Ethiopian sovereignty (Collins,1983). On the other hand, British officials in Sudan strongly disagreed with Ethiopian claims of Sudanese citizens as subjects of the Ethiopian Emperor. British knew that in the agreement of 1902, Anuak was the only tribe divided into two countries, but not Nuer. The colonial officials were shocked to learn that an Ethiopian military officer could arrogantly claim that Nuers were Ethiopian citizens. "Never in the history of the eastern frontier had an Ethiopian official ever made such a demand," said Collins.

Despite Sudanese rejection of Ethiopian claims, Majid continued with this 'Ethiopianization' policy. Collins (1983) revealed that Majid appointed Koryom Tut, a chief of Gaajak Nuer, to convince his fellow Nuer to accept Ethiopian citizenship. The appointment of Koryom angered Gaajak Nuer, who rejected the Ethiopians claims on his people. To prove they were not Ethiopians, the Nuers refused to pay taxes to the Ethiopian government. As a result of their disagreements, about 300 Gaajak Nuers attacked Kurthony (Collins,1983). This was a clear indication that Nuer people fought to remain free from Ethiopian control and taxation because they were not Ethiopian citizens at all. "The incident clearly demonstrated the deteriorating situation on the frontier and the need for a local agreement over grazing between Sudan and Ethiopia," Collins said.

It is important to remember that the British had been supporting Ethiopian expansion since 1902. This meant that Ethiopian people relied on British support to colonise other nations neighbouring Ethiopia. Consequently, Ras Mulugeta, an Ethiopian official agreed to negotiate with the Sudanese official for a grazing land agreement (Collins, 1983). To settle the grazing land agreement, the Sudanese government proposed to pay fees for grazing land in Ethiopia. For that reason, the Governor of Upper Nile, Pawson, agreed to negotiate the grazing land agreement for Nuers' cattle. The Sudanese government paid grazing fees to the Ethiopian authorities in recognition of Nuer people as the Sudanese tribe (Collins,1983).

About the same time, Mulugeta was called to Addis Ababa before he met with the British officials in Sudan. After his departure, Majid Abud was left in charge of the frontier affairs, but he refused to negotiate a grazing agreement with Sudanese officials (Collins,1983). Thus, with the lack of evidence to prove the Nuers' citizenship in Ethiopia, Majid avoided meeting the Sudanese people to negotiate the deal. Instead, he tried to convince the Nuer directly, bypassing the Sudanese government because he knew that they would not agree with his claim. He continued his plan, without shame. "But he sent his agents among the Nuer chiefs to urge them with a combination of sweet talk, threats, and bribes to transfer their allegiance to the emperor," Collins writes. Again, Majid's claims were rejected by the Sudanese government.

Majid Abud made a similar mistake as the British did, 31 years earlier. The British and Ethiopians signed an agreement in 1902 (Collins, 1983). It was another unjustifiable error. History and territorial ownership made Majid's claims strongly unrealistic. First, Anuak people had lived on both sides of the Akobo river for centuries before the British came and divided them. In the agreement of 1902, Akobo was used to separate Anuaks into two countries. Second, Nuers discovered by Majid, not in their own land to be claimed as Ethiopians. However, Nuer people grazed their cattle in Anuak locations in the Gambella region usually without permission. Third, all tribes that lived in Ethiopia, each had their own land before it was incorporated into the Ethiopian federation. Therefore, his claim of Nuers as Ethiopians was ignorant and astonishing: a new tribe could not be discovered in the Anuak kingdom.

It is important to understand the relationships between Anuak and Nuer! Both tribes are South Sudanese citizens and they lived close to each other in South Sudan. But Nuer people are not Ethiopians. South Sudanese Anuaks and Ethiopian Anuaks are living on the borderline, respectively. According to Collins (1983) Majid's claim showed that Nuer people were grazing their cattle between Anuaks' villages during the dry season. As a foreigner in Anuak land, Majid assumed that Nuer pastoralists lived in those locations. But Anuak people allowed them to come to Dikony, Bur-Obey, Adura and Openo rivers in search of water for their cattle. In the rainy season, Nuer people returned to their home villages in Southern Sudan. More importantly, when there is peace between the two communities, an Anuak community that borders the Nuers would let them come to their villages for drinking water and green pastures for their cattle, temporarily. Due to those agreements, Nuers brought their cows to the Ethiopian side even though they were not living in those locations permanently (Collins,1983). Evaluating Majid claims of Nuers as Ethiopians, it revealed that in 1933, Anuaks were living in Jokaw and Akobo under the British administration. There was no Nuer living between Anuak of Southern Sudan and Anuak of Ethiopia in Gambella.

Third Ethiopian Incursion to Gambella

In May 1934, Majid Abud returned to Gambella as an imperial agent to set up an Ethiopian administration office (Collins, 1983). The headman of Itang, Ray Gillo, was unhappy with the Ethiopian expansion into the Openo region where he lived. When he came to power, Ray demarcated the Anuak-Opo border, according to Obang. On the northern border, there were Oromo people. **Kewa-Kidi** means 'our natural border with Oromo people is the mountain'. The boundaries between the Anuak people and their neighbouring tribes were drawn. The Kwar political system has existed for thousands of years in Anuak society and a map of the entire Anuak nation was drawn to prevent foreigners and invaders from stealing Anuak lands. The notion of border protection was based on the ancient rules of Cuai. Thus, when someone crossed the border without permission, he violated the sovereignty of another nation. Since Ethiopian forces invaded Gambella, Ray had the right to defend the territorial integrity of the Anuak people.

As a result of the invasion, on 26 May 1934, Anuak people of Itang attacked the Ethiopian forces killing sixty soldiers on the spot and dispersed them from their base in the Openo region. At this time, Majid Abud was severely wounded in the fighting (Collins,1983, p. 80). "He brought with him several hundred men and machine guns. To his astonishment, while collecting taxes, his men were attacked by a large number of the Baro (Openo) Anuak and were nearly overwhelmed. Only his machine gun saved him from disaster; his men scattered, and many were killed on the spot. They retreated to Gambella where he and his forces stayed. He would have been annihilated had it not been for his police officers from Gambella, who rescued the wounded Majid," Collins stated. According to him, during the fight, the military officer lost almost everything. "Majid lost everything—baggage, ammunition, guns, large quantities of currency," Collins said.

When the British understood the strength of the Anuaks, they started to doubt the Ethiopian ability to control them. The last defeat of the Ethiopian forces proved the British scepticism about its ally's military capability. At the same time, the Ethiopians defeat reminded the British of their own defeat at the hands of the Anuak people in Sudan in 1912. After the Ethiopians defeat in the last battle, the British realised that the Ethiopian government was too weak to succeed in administering the Anuak people in Ethiopia (Collins, 1983). It also proved that Ray Gillo would not allow his people to live under the jurisdiction of the Ethiopian Kingdom.

Ethiopians Bring Nuers Into The Game

Foreign political interests complicated everything in Anuak land. According to Obang, another security concern in the Openo region was that of the Nuer bringing their cattle to Itang during the dry seasons. Nyium (Nasir) was one of the Anuak regions that the Nuer people invaded in the 1850 (Collins,1983). Nuers invaded Anuak land 30 years before Anuaks obtained guns. However, the Nuers were contained in the Nyium region while Anuaks planned to take it back. After the acquisition of firearms by King Odiel Kwot in 1880, Anuaks prepared to push the Nuers from their land. At that time, there were no Nuer people in Ethiopia. But Majid's claim brought them to live in Anuak territory in Ethiopia, according to Collins. As a result, some Nuers came to Anuak villages on the Openo river. Some Anuak communities welcomed Nuers to stay, temporarily, for the dry season, to return to their homes after rainfall. As a pastoralist community, Nuer people moved to the Anuak areas for water and green pastures.

Obang stated that an agreement was made with the Nuer to bring their cattle, goats, and sheep to Itang, but they had to pay grazing fees. Likewise, conditions and terms of the agreements spelled out clearly for both parties to follow: All protocols must be observed. This suggested that any violation of the agreements would lead to eviction of the Nuer seasonal migrants from Itang. Apparently, agreements signed with Nuer people never lasted because they failed to obey the rules. "Those Nuer people who moved to Itang violated terms of the agreement; they started hunting, fishing, pounding grain and sitting on animal skins where Anuak men were sitting," Obang said. According to Anuak people in Itang, it was forbidden for naked Nuer to sit on the skins reserved for the Anuak men and considered a violation of the agreement. During that period, some Nuer men went to take baths in the river where men were not allowed to bathe. For example, Nuer women were allowed to take baths where Anuak women bathed, but Nuer men went to take a bath in the women's designated bathing areas. This was considered disrespectful of Anuak women. It seemed Nuers did not care about the rules and Anuak men could not tolerate such violations of their culture. The Nuers' cows were out of control, eating crops or destroying maize in the farms that belonged to Anuak people. This was a serious violation of the agreements that both parties had signed, according to Obang. So, Anuaks prepared to address grazing land problems immediately. Ray Gillo called an emergency meeting in Bura with his top advisors. Members of Bura concluded that their agreement for water usage was not respected. Prior to the water agreement, Itang warned Nuers to keep their cows, goats and sheep far from the farms. Two months later, Nuers' cattle were on the farms!

The destruction of crops was reported to the headman, Ray Gillo. An official report from Bura gave more details to Ray's administration concerning destruction of maize, sorghum, hunting and fishing in forbidden places, according to Obang. For example, fishing or hunting was forbidden in holy places. After receiving the reports at Bura, the case was transferred to Kwach-Lwak, the general Chief of staff of Itang forces for further investigation.

An investigation was conducted, and it was followed by a series of meetings to resolve the situation. Eventually, the people of Itang agreed to take military action against the Nuers after peaceful efforts failed, he revealed. The Anuaks met the Nuer where Ray explained grievances and how important it was for the two communities to live in peace. Ray said it was the generosity of Itang's people that allowed strangers to come to their homes for humanitarian reasons. To live in the host community, Nuers should follow protocols of the agreement. Ray Gillo told them any deviation from the agreement should result in eviction or military action. "At the meeting, fighting erupted between Nuers and Anuaks; Nuers were defeated and chased out from Anuak land," Obang said.

After the heavy fighting ended, the Sudanese government negotiated with Ethiopian government and the meeting resolved to force Anuak headmen to live with Nuers whether they liked it or not. As stated before, every agreement between British and Ethiopian was always to diminish power of the Anuak people. A governor of Illubabor in Ethiopia sent a delegation to Gambella and called Anuak chiefs and kings to attend the meeting, according to Obang. Even though Anuak leaders rejected Ethiopians' proposal to bring Nuer people to their land, Ethiopians signed the grazing agreement without consent of the Anuaks. "As a result, the agreement was signed which allowed Nuer people to come to Anuak land because Ethiopian government forced the Anuak people to live with Nuers," he said. A few months later, after the agreement was signed, Ethiopian Emperor Haile Selassie invited Koryom Tut to Addis Ababa (Collins, 1983). In the meeting held with the Ethiopian leaders, Haile Selassie persuaded Koryom to claim Nuers were Ethiopians, according to Collins.

But this contradicted the agreement signed by the two countries! Now, Koryom Tut, who was appointed by Majid Abud to promote an 'Ethiopianisation' agenda, was persuading Nuer people to become Ethiopians (Collins, 1983). With Ethiopian support and political manipulation, the Nuers started to move to Jokaw, an Anuak town in Southern Sudan, to occupy land on the Ethiopian side as well. To ensure the smooth implementation of the grazing land agreement signed between the two countries, the Ethiopian government brought police and the army to Gambella City—this was the time the Ethiopian government came to Gambella to undermine Anuak political power in their land. Despite inconsistencies in the agreement, the British ignored and supported the deception plan.

Europeans took advantage of traditional rivalry among the African tribes according to Kevin. From 1902 to 1936, the British and its Ethiopian ally imposed their artificial boundary between the Anuak people, forcing them to live in both Ethiopia and Sudan (Kevin, 2012). The agreement favoured the Nuer to occupy Anuak land! British considered Anuaks an obstacle in East Africa. To succeed in its colonisation, they believed the Anuaks' military power should be diminished in order to subdue them. Anuak leaders, since their acquisition of firearms, would not give up. Two kings, Odiel and Olimi, attacked Jikany Nuer who lived in the Anuak territory. Later, King Akway Cham cleared both Lou Nuer and Jikany Nuer out of the Anuak land in 1911 (Evans-Pritchard, 1940). After those attacks, Nuers abandoned the land where they settled in the previous years, according to Evans-Pritchard. Unfortunately, since Nuers were British subjects in Southern Sudan, their masters intervened, supporting them militarily, but British forces suffered a shock loss to King Akway Cham at the Battle of Juom. After all, without British intervention, there would be no Nuers living in Anuak land today! It was the British plan to destroy the Anuak independent nation in multiple ways. The damage the British created in 1902 is still negatively affecting the Anuak people today!

Italian Invasion of Ethiopia

Political enemies in Europe competed against each other for an African nation they both claimed: Panywaa. The Italian invasion of Ethiopia in 1936 radically changed the agreement of 1902: The Anglo-Egyptian Sudan feared that Italian authority in Ethiopia would control water flow from upstream (Collins,1983). The British looked for options to alleviate their fear of water blockage when the Italians decided to use water for irrigation or other purposes. "On 3 October 1935, Italian troops crossed the Eritrean frontier, reaching Makele in early November," Collins wrote. They soon advanced toward the

Ethiopian capital, Addis Ababa. Kevin (2012) stated that Italian forces pushed their way to Addis Ababa with victory in every battle. One day before the Italian forces entered Addis Ababa, Emperor Haile Selassie fled into exile in Europe for his personal safety, according to Kevin. "On May 4, Haile Selassie left Addis Ababa the following day, Marshal Pietro Badoglio entered the capital," Kevin reported.

Just eight months later, an Italian expedition arrived in Gambella. The Italian mission was to conquer Ethiopia for its colony. "On December 17, 1936, two Italian generals, twelve officers, and 100 Italian troops motored to Gambella with planes overhead," Collins said. Further, Gambella was an important town for both European colonisers because it allowed trading between the Sudanese and people who lived in Western Ethiopia. In this case, each European power wanted to control Gambella for its own interests. To settle their dispute over Gambella, the British and the Italians made another agreement regarding their interests in the Anuak land. Once again, the Anuak people were completely ignored and left out in the agreement signed by two European imperialists.

12

The Agreement of The Olimi Triangle

Olimi Akwon was an Anuak king who lived in Okwa in the Tiernam region. According to Collins, the Olimi Triangle was named after the Anuak leader. In this agreement, the British acknowledged that the previous agreement of 1902 failed to study boundaries between the two countries: Paanywaa and Ethiopia. In the old agreement, the British blindly believed that Anuak people were Ethiopians. As they established colonial offices in Pochalla and Akobo, the British learned more about the Anuaks and their geographical locations. In Gambella, they recognised the natural border between Ethiopians and the Anuaks. Amazingly, things that the British did not see from a distance became conspicuous on the ground. Consequently, the Anglo-Italian agreement, which was signed on 16 April 1938, gave Gambella to the British. While the Italians kept Ethiopian land on the top of the mountain and the British on the bottom of it, Gambella became a Sudanese territory (Collins, 1983). The Anglo-Italian treaty used Kewa-kidi as their international border. They accepted the natural border known to Oromo and Anuak communities. As mentioned earlier, the British changed its policies drastically due to perceived fear of the

Italian government controlling the flow of water from Ethiopia. The solution was to keep the Italians out of Gambella, according to Collins. This meant that all Anuaks became Sudanese citizens.

"To abandon it (Gambella) to the Italians would not only damage British prestige but would seal off the only outlet for western Ethiopia to the outside world," Collins reported.

Impact of Political Change in Europe

Victors of World War II took the colonies of other European countries that lost the war. After clearing the Italian troops out of Gambella during World War II, the British realised that it was time to take Gambella into Sudan. By December 1941, Gambella was annexed to Sudan (Collins, 1983). From that year, Gambellan Anuaks who were claimed by Ethiopians in the 1902 agreement became Sudanese citizens. The old agreement between Emperor Menelik and Anglo-Egyptian Sudan was replaced by the new agreement that gave Gambella to Sudan. Each agreement determining where Anuak people belonged was always done without their participation in the decision-making. The European powers worked hard to weaken Anuak authority in their nation! Due to deception and prejudice against the Anuaks, the British initially gave Gambella to Ethiopia. In other words, Anuak land was given to Ethiopians to build their relations. At the same time, the British planned to fight the Sudanese people who resisted colonialism in Khartoum. In their agreements, Anuaks became victims of foreign interests in the region (Collins, 1983). Nevertheless, the Anglo Italian agreement was not the end of the abuse, political manipulation, and division of the Anuaks at the hands of foreigners. After fifteen years as Sudanese people, the last agreement to give Gambella back to Ethiopia was signed in October 1956 by the Sudanese and Ethiopian governments. The deal was made ten months after Sudan gained its independence from the British (Collins, 1983).

The latest agreement between Ethiopian and Sudanese governments separated Anuak people on the British artificial boundary using Akobo river. The Anuak people went through multiple citizenships without giving them an opportunity to choose their own destiny. Eventually, in the October agreement of 1956, Anuaks were permanently split between Ethiopia and Sudan (Collins, 1983). This has had a disastrous impact on the Anuak people for 119 years (1902 to the present day) and an example of the most extreme exploitation. This exploitation needs to be rectified to ensure that the Anuaks live in their own sovereign country of Paanywaa. Anuak people need to choose their own destiny—whether to be Ethiopians, South Sudanese, or to restore their own independent state. Their separation by the British and its allies was the leading cause of the destruction of the once powerful nation in the African continent. For the Anuak people to be free again from foreign manipulation and exploitation, restoration of Paanywaa nation is the solution!

13

The Headmen of Ciro State

Ciro is the western part of Paanywaa, neighbouring Nyium to the north, and it borders Lou Nuer to the west. Akobo is the capital of Ciro state. It is the second region after Nyium that dealt with Nuer invasions according to Evans-Pritchard. However, during the acquisition of firearms in the 1880s, Anuaks were able to push Nuer people back to their homeland. Evans-Pritchard (1940) stated that King Akway-War-Cham, in 1911, led a counter raid against the Nuers twice. His counterattacks devastated both Nuer Lou and Jikany Nuer. After the military mission was accomplished, King Akway returned to Adongo taking hundreds of cattle from the Nuer. Evans-Pritchard (1940) reported that a similar raid was carried out by Anuaks from Ciro, attacking a group of Nuers who lived closer to Akobo and pushed them out from the Anuak land.

Interview with Hon. Barnaba Okony Gillo, conducted on 23 November 2019 on conflict between Anuak and Nuer in Akobo County.

According to Hon. Barnaba, finding a peaceful solution is the key for both communities to live peacefully. He is a prominent politician who represented Anuak people in Akobo county in Jonglei state. He served as a Minister of Health from 2014 and 2016. Barnaba strongly oppose the domination of Nuers in the representation of Akobo. He noted that Nuers took all parliamentary seats in the national government in Juba. He said those seats should be divided between Anuak and Nuer equally. As a representative of the Anuaks in Akobo, he was fighting for political fairness and equal representation of the Anuak people at the state level and national government in Juba.

Barnaba provided extensive details about the arrival of the Nuers in Akobo. The Nuer immigrants were welcomed by the Anuak community in Akobo. Anuaks allowed them to live in Akobo territory. According to him, both communities co-existed peacefully in the past. In 1912, there was a big flood in Akobo. As a result, the town was transferred to the current Akobo town. Before the British arrived in Sudan and during colonial rule, Anuak people were living in Ciro and Nyium regions. In the Anuak political system, there was no border between Ciro and Nyium. Similarly, Nyium and Openo were connected. It showed that there was no single Nuer village between Anuak regions. All those three regions—Ciro, Nyium and Openo—were connected, according to Barnaba. Furthermore, boundaries among Anuak regions allowed free movement from one region to another. This suggested that people travelled freely to places they wanted to go to. Meanwhile, Anuaks knew their borders with every state including landowners of each village that made up the Anuak nation.

There were appropriate land policies and regulations in the Anuak nation. Hence, land dispute among the Anuak people was rare because every clan had their own land in their ancestral homes. Landowners allowed non-members of their clan to live in their villages, but immigrants could not claim ownership of the land. This policy was respected by all Anuaks. The land was not for sale except in rare situations. Additionally, Anuaks knew their borders with their neighbouring tribes. They applied the same boundary rules, which they used internally between their states. Thus, Anuak leaders enforced boundary policies effectively so that violators could be held accountable and pay fines.

Evans-Pritchard (p. 48) noted the function of Kwac Ngom, or landowner, was to pray for soil productivity, fish abundance and safety of the fishermen. This confirmed that all landowners had the right to keep their land. Similarly, when crossing boundaries on farms where big problems might occur, the boundary was respected, and permission was sought first. All farmers knew the surrounding clans and communities and other farmers who ploughed the land. It meant everyone knew how big or small an individual farm was and who owned the land. To ensure that nobody crossed the line, a type of plant called **Apitoo** that looked like an onion, was planted between individual's farms to demarcate borders between the two farmlands (Evans-Pritchard,1940). So, when a farmer crossed into another person's farm, it was considered a crime. If two farmers failed to resolve their boundary dispute, they would take the case to a higher level—at Bura where it would be addressed by the headman or at Poor by the king, depending on where the individuals lived. Clearly, a violator pays a fine for his actions of taking land from someone else's farm. Violators were also forced legally to return the land to its rightful owners. Due to this rule and its severe consequences, Anuaks were aware of their borders with all tribes. For instance, Anuak people in Adongo, Tiernam, and Ojwa regions, knew their borders with Murle people. Likewise, Anuak people in Ciro and Nyium knew exactly where their boundaries were with the Nuer people. There was a clear demarcated boundary between Anuaks and the Nuers. Yet, Nuers kept crossing the boundary between the two nations.

The British and Anuak monarchs have similar land policies! In the Anuak federation, land belongs to the clans. More importantly, British established land boundaries among all tribes in Southern Sudan. Before they left Sudan after independence, British demarcated boundaries among all Southern Sudanese tribes on 1 January 1956. "In 1956, British created a boundary at Adawa-Achan between Anuak of Ciro and Nuer Lou," Barnaba said. The tribal boundaries showed where each tribe lived in Southern Sudan during British rule in Sudan. It was the best way to prevent land grabbing in South Sudan. Those boundaries were not only important for South Sudanese people to stop land grabbing, but they were also a demarcated international boundary between South Sudan and North Sudan as two separate states.

Nuer Immigrants Asked for a Settlement in Akobo

According to Barnaba, the first Nuer groups asked Okway-Wara-Ading for settlement in his village. Okway Ading was one of the headmen in the Ciro region, and he knew that he was not the landowner of the village where he resided. But the landowner of his homestead lived in another place. Allowing Nuers to live in Okway's residency required consultation with the landowner. The land belonged to Otheri-Wara-Ajack, he said. During that time, Othiri Ajack was living in Dimma village in Akobo. While Okway-Winychuro was the headman of Dikole, he lived on the bank of Keng river! There were various headmen from different villages in Ciro, but one of them was the paramount chief for the whole region. Barnaba asserted that Jok-Wara-Ajer was the paramount chief recognised by Anglo-Egyptian Sudan's government. He was the leader of Anuak political affairs in Ciro. After consultation was made, Anuak leaders accepted Nuer people to live in Akobo.

Nuer Families Moved to Akobo

Anuak people love and care deeply for their fellow humans. They welcomed the newcomers to their homes and treated them with dignity. The Anuak are the natives of Akobo who have lived in the Ciro state since the fifteenth century. Yet their hospitality and generosity enabled Nuer immigrants to live in the Anuak community. When Nuers came to Akobo, they were only a few families and initially lived peacefully with the Anuak people. Decades of co-existence with the Nuers showed that they were peaceful only when Nuers were a minority in Anuak land. But later, Nuers abused the hospitality of their host. When their population grew in Akobo, the Nuers turned violent and murderous. In fact, the first Nuer people to arrive in Nyium were peaceful, but good relations ended violently. Historical facts suggest that Nuer bellicose occurred when they became the majority in the areas in which they lived.

The first Nuer immigrants who moved to Akobo from Lou Nuer were only five families, according to Barnaba. "An estimated population of Nuer people in Akobo in 1931 was 800. While the Ciro-Anuak population was 25,000," he said. In 1931, Anuaks were living in thirty-seven villages with a population of 25,000. Since Nuers were a minority in the Anuak community, their families were known to Anuak people in Akobo. The Anuak headmen in Akobo assisted Nuers to settle in certain locations. Due to these arrangements, five families of Nuer immigrants were accepted to live in the following places:

1: Lual Thian settled in Dikon-Battkek (Kaibui).
2: Kok Diang was taken to Deng Jwok Village.
3: Nyieng Chamjok and his family lived in Bur-Mer.
(Those three villages were the first places in Akobo to welcome Nuer immigrants, he said.)
4: A Nuer magician went to King Agada Akway in Otalo and asked him to

stay in Akobo. The king told him to talk to the leaders of Akobo regarding settlement in their region. Barnaba stated that after the Nuer magician came from Otalo, he asked Ciro's leaders for a settlement, which was approved by the Anuak leaders in Akobo.

5: The last group of Nuer immigrants was the family of Kot Wal, the father Tap Kode settled in Bur-Mer.

James Ochang Ojoch is one of the elders in the Anuak community and a former Director for Agriculture in Jonglei State. He added that the drought of 1948 brought another group of Nuer to Akobo for water reasons. A British commissioner in Waat made a temporary agreement with another British commissioner in Akobo in 1948 to allow Nuer people to come to Akobo during the months of drought in the Nuerland. However, those Nuers ended up staying in Akobo permanently, James stated.

Missionaries Arrived in Akobo

American missionaries built a church in Akobo in 1948! The first American missionary in Akobo was Harvey Hoekstra (Odola Otoura) followed by Don McClure (Odan). Both men were given Anuak names when they lived in Akobo. They were known as Odola and Odan, throughout their missionary work in Anuak land. First, Odan learnt the Anuak language. In the following years, he translated the Bible into Anuak language. Barnaba said that Odan completed the New Testament in the Anuak language which enabled the spread of Christian faith among the Anuak people in the 1950s. Odan's dedication helped Anuaks to study the Bible in their native language! Today, Anuak people give much credit to Odan.

Church Indoctrination

In chapter one of this book, Diop (1989) stated that Egypt was the centre for political and religious ideologies. All Western countries learnt the concept of religion from the Anu or Anuak people in Egypt. According to Diop, for Greeks to understand God, God was reduced to the level of man for them to understand. But in the Anuak society, God is the spirit not a man. It cannot be drawn like a man. It is omnipresent. As colonial powers implemented White ideology, missionaries promoted their religion among non-whites in Africa. The primary purpose was to spread Christianity and acquire more members of their faith in Africa and to make them relinquish any African religion in favour of Christianity. "In 1940-1950 a primary school was opened in Akobo in Anuak language," Barnaba stated. Since the school opened in Anuak land, anyone who lived in Akobo town studied the Anuak language in school.

Education is the best way to increase humans' capacity in science, mathematics, politics, technology and so forth. It is the brain power that liberates students from uncritical ways of thinking and reasoning. The first educated Anuaks began their primary school in Akobo. It was the only school in Anuak land in Sudan. There was no high school anywhere in the Anuak community in Sudan. Today the same is true. From 2005 to 2021, no high school has been built either in Akobo or Pochalla. The first prominent Anuaks who went to Akobo school became well known in the entire Sudan. These include Professor/Politician Paul Anade Othow, Ambassador Philip Obang Ojway, Engineer Ochan Agwa, Teacher Cham Adhom, and Politician Simon Mori Didumo. This school produced the bravest and wisest men who founded Anya-Nya 1 Movement in the Upper Nile region in 1962: Paul Nyingory Ojulu, Andrew Thowl Cham, and Stephen Ogut Obongo. In addition, Joseph Oteo Akwon led the movement, after Paul Nyinglory was removed from power in 1968, until his death in 1972, just to mention a few. All these Anuak intellectuals and military leaders attended primary school in Akobo.

After British lost the war in the Adongo region in 1912, relations between British and Anuaks were hostile. British considered that educating Anuaks would be dangerous as they were already civilized. Anuaks had political power to keep British forces out of their land and they had knowledge that could free a person from mental slavery and physical control. The British did not want Anuaks to go to higher education because they believed they were born with knowledge and skills. So, the British convinced Sudanese and Ethiopian governments not to open schools in Anuak land beyond primary schools. Above all, the British believed that educated Anuaks would be too powerful for them to control in Sudan and Ethiopia.

There was only one school in Akobo district and Nuers sent their children to school in Akobo town. Barnaba explained that: "In 1952, Nuer people asked Anuaks to allow their children to be educated in the Anuak language in Akobo." The Anuak leaders in Ciro agreed to these children studying in Akobo school. That was one of the reasons which brought Nuers to Akobo! Some Nuers who were educated in Anuak language held ministerial posts in Salva Kiir's administration. "The first educated Nuer man in Anuak language was John Luk Jok, a former minister of justice in South Sudan," Barnaba said. He was not alone! There were many Nuer people who were educated in the Anuak language: Dr. Riek Gai Kok, former Minister of Health in the central government in Juba, Timothy Taban Juch, a former Governor of defunct Akobo state in 2020, Tayeen Kok Diang, and Achol Luak Kok – all those people were sons and a daughter of the Nuers who moved to Akobo from Lou Nuer.

Conflict Between Anuak and Nuer in Akobo

Welcoming strangers to your house can be a source of conflict that destroys the very house strangers are welcomed. Hospitality and friendship of the Anuaks shown to the Nuers soured with the Nuers' violent behaviours on one side and Anuak's peaceful manners on the other. "Anuak people welcomed Nuer people to settle in Akobo, mainly in three villages," Barnaba said. The two tribes lived peacefully from 1948 to 1973. In 1973, relations between the two tribes began to deteriorate after the Addis Ababa agreement in 1972. Some Nuer politicians destroyed peaceful co-existence between Anuak and Nuer communities. Both communities still remembered their peaceful relations when they lived side by side peacefully for nearly three decades. The problems in Akobo were created by the sons and grandchildren of the Nuer who migrated to Akobo from Lou Nuer. They planned to push Anuaks out of their land. The Anuak and Nuer communities needed to find peaceful solutions to a conflict that has lasted for more than 48 years until the present day. "When King Akway Cham attacked the Nuers in 1911, the Nuers returned to their land," Barnaba stated. Before developing tribal hatred, these two communities had peaceful relations in the previous decades. During that period, members of both communities moved back and forth safely, according to Barnaba.

Anuak's Meet with Ngundeng Bong

Nuer immigrants in Akobo told a fascinating story about Ngundeng to the Anuak people! He was considered a prophet by the Nuer people. During conversations with the Nuer people in Akobo, Anuaks heard about Ngundeng. To find out the truth about him, Owar Nyigwo, an Anuak man, and his friends decided to go to the village where Ngundeng lived in Lou Nuer land. Owar who lived in Akobo with Nuers became interested in the story, and he wanted to know whether Ngundeng existed. He was thrilled to see Ngundeng for himself.

Owar was a famous blacksmith in Akobo! He was curious about Ngundeng and made him a smoking pipe as a surprise gift. At home in Akobo, Owar knew that Nuer smokers used traditional pipes, which were made of mud or clay. He planned to make a special pipe that looked better and felt different. He made Ngundeng a smoking pipe with metal which was the best quality. When Owar finished, he went to Nuer land with friends to meet with Ngundeng. What Owar did for Ngundeng is still remembered by Nuer people today. When Owar presented the surprise gift to Ngundeng upon his arrival in the village, Ngundeng could not believe that Anuak men travelled so far to offer him a special gift. To honour the friendly relations between the two communities, Anuak people were welcomed in Lou Nuer. Meanwhile, Ngundeng was so excited and he personally scooped butter to feed Owar!

However, Nuers who were sitting with him, said that the scoop was too big for one man. They complained that giving a big gourd full of butter to one man was more likely to finish the butter they had. Overall, Ngundeng was very happy with his new smoking pipe. He was fascinated by the luxury gift from the Anuak people who came to see him. The special gift signified peace and love among brothers and an analogy for the two tribes to live as brothers.

14

Anuak Marriage: Nywom

Marriages, weddings, and social gatherings are important events in Anuak society. Anuaks value and enjoy events that bring both women and men together in celebration. According to Anuak tradition, marriage is a vital union that unites a man and woman through love. As a polygamist society, a man can marry more than one wife and live with them in the same house. Their marriage requires the groom to pay a bride price or bride-wealth to the family of the bride. Nearly every Anuak man or woman who fits the marriageable age is married. There are three types of marriages in the Anuak culture—**Cood, Nywom,** and **Biel**. Each type of marriage is unique in its function and meaning. Regardless of the definition or mode of marriage, payment of bride wealth is required for all marriages. More importantly, it is the bride wealth that legitimises the marriage. For that reason, failure to pay bride wealth results in marriage denial and cancellation by the bride's father. Learning different vocabularies about marriage enables a man to choose which one best suits him.

Cood (Courtship) An Anuak couple develops a romantic relationship that builds mutual understanding before getting married. Cood is the most popular marriage in the Anuak society. At the age of 16-17, Anuak boys and girls start dating. Youths have many social gatherings where they meet one another and interact. Most of the social events that attract young people are weddings and Bul (drum dance). During these events, young people have opportunities to meet new friends and get acquainted. In the modern day, schools and churches are the new places for singles to meet. As boys and girls meet, some boys may find certain girls attractive to them. So, they start communicating! It is the beginning of developing friendship, which may turn to an intimate relationship or it may end up in marriage.

In the older generation, dating takes between six months to a year, or longer. First the relation between the male and female is not known to the public. Anuak people have a tradition of keeping their relationships secret in the beginning, although some trusted friends will know who their friends are dating. They want to ensure that they develop a relationship that shows genuine love, friendship, happiness, and commitment. Boys and girls choose their intimate partners. Due to the freedom of Cood for girls, it is the most popular mode of marriage in Anuak culture. Therefore, the majority of the Anuaks' marriages begin with courtship. After a relationship has been established, members of the girl's family want to find out if their daughter is dating someone. During this time, parents may have heard information about their daughter's boyfriend, or they acknowledge that she is at the marriageable age.

Culturally, when Anuak girls reach a marriageable age, their parents have the right to know who their daughter's boyfriend is. The parents of the girl want to know who is courting their daughter so they can start investigating his background. The girl's father directs her brothers or young men of the family to speak with their sister and find out if she is dating and with whom. They will ask her if she is in a relationship. As a rule, girls, at first, deny any relationship. But her brothers would insist that they need to know who her boyfriend is and will persist until she says. Usually, girls will ask to be given between one or two weeks to report back to them. In this period, the girl talks to her boyfriend and they discuss the way forward, before she introduces him to the family.

This is a critical time for the girl or woman as there is uncertainty in this process: a girl could be denied or abandoned by her boyfriend, who does not want to take the relationship further. After permission from her brothers, the girl arranges a face-to-face private talk with her boyfriend. Once she confirms that her boyfriend is committed to their relationship, he then proposes to marry her. Congratulations! This is the time an Anuak girl reveals the name and identity of her boyfriend to her family. Thus, the Anuak dating rules of communication between girlfriends and boyfriends is followed before a report is given to the family.

There are positive and negative outcomes of these relationships before marriage. For instance, a positive outcome means that the girl's boyfriend is interested in marrying her. He tells his girlfriend he is in love with her, and he wants to get married. On the other hand, he may reject her with a denial of having had any intimate relations with the female. There are consequences for a man who dates a girl but denies her later. The man can be severely punished for falsely being in a relationship that does not lead to marriage.

Hence, before dating occurs between, each party brings a friend as a representative; the friend is a witness and also speaks on their behalf in the early days of the relationship. This is to ensure that in the case of rejection by the male, each spokesperson will testify to confirm whether the relationship did in fact take place or not. So, when the boyfriend denies the intimate relations with the girl he has been dating, he is more likely to be beaten up. But the woman is free to walk away from a relationship without consequences.

How does a woman know that a man she is dating will not commit to a long-term relationship? Dating without an intention to get married follows its own rules. The first indication that the relationship is only temporary, is when there are no other people involved. There are few things that determine whether the relationship would last: When friends are introduced to both parties. Also, when the female gives her boyfriend **Cang -Caa**, a type of bracelet made of beads and a bead necklace. This is affirming their love for each other and a confirmation of their strong relationship! When the girlfriend gives these beads to her boyfriend, this is her way of letting him know that she is in love with him. However, when her boyfriend denies the relationship later, he would be in trouble. The friends from each side will confirm the authenticity of the relationship. Once a relationship is confirmed by the girl's family, they will demand that the boyfriend come to them. If he does not come, they will go to his house and reprimand him. The man will be brought to the family of the girl for questioning. If the relationship is proven, he will be forced to pay bride wealth. However, if the boyfriend willingly comes to the family, negotiations take place between his family and the family of the girlfriend to come to a suitable arrangement. After all, **Cood** marriage has the lowest number of marriage rejections due to the time both partners invest in the relationships and most are based on love.

Nywom: If a man wants to marry a woman, he sends his friends or relatives to the father of the woman to inform him of his interest in marriage. It means that the suitor wishes to marry a lady he has not dated or had intimate relationship with. In doing so, he declares his intentions to the family of the girl to marry her whether he is engaged or not. There are two types of Nywom definitions: First a man proposes to marry a lady he does not have a relationship with. In this case, he sends his friends to the bride's family informing them that he is interested in marrying the girl. The second type of Nywom, is similar to Cood except the man visits his girlfriend's family and declares his intention to marry. The second type of Nywom is more acceptable usually because the couple know each other and have been dating. Now, the boyfriend has made a commitment to marry his sweetheart.

In both types of Nywom, it is the choice of the woman to accept or reject the proposal. If she agrees to the marriage, her father will approve. But if the woman rejects the marriage proposal her father will support her decision. Once Nywom has been declined, it will not take place. It is easier for the second type of Nywom to be accepted by the woman since she has been in a relationship with the boyfriend. Nywom is the opposite of Cood. With Cood, the bride informs her father about her boyfriend either willingly or after questioning by her father and relatives. While with Nywom, the man goes to the father of the bride notifying him that he wants to marry his daughter.

However, some women will agree to marry men who ask their families even though they may not know them. This method is often used by older men or young men who live far away from the woman. In a Nywom marriage, the man intending to marry the woman sends a messenger known as **Nyi-Joo**, who will go to the house of the bride's father to talk to them. The messenger would request an appropriate time to meet and disclose the reason. The father of the lady and his relatives meet to discuss the marriage proposal. They will deliberate on the background and family history of the man. The background check determines if the couple from the two clans are appropriate to marry each other. One of the things they discus is whether members of the bridegroom's family dated and rejected a girl from the bride's family or clan in the past. This information is critical for the parents of the bride to know! They also discuss whether there has been bloodshed or animosity between the two clans in the past. Another important aspect of the discussion is whether the couple are relatives because members of the same clan or family are forbidden from marrying each other in Anuak culture. After the family completes their deliberation, they arrange a proper time to meet the man's family. The father of the bride will send his own messenger to communicate their availability to meet the bridegroom's family. Both families meet face-to-face to approve marriage and settle bride wealth payments. Most marriage proposals are accepted, but some girls may reject marriage from men they do not know.

In studying a Nywom proposal, it shows that women have the power to accept or reject marriage proposals. It is intimacy in relationship, courtship, dating or love that attaches couples to each other, socially and emotionally. This is the reason some marriage proposals are easily accepted, while others are strongly rejected. Girls make decisions about who to marry! Most Anuak girls do not marry strangers or unknown men! Due to this attitude, prior to accepting a marriage, a father informs his daughter about the man who is proposing marriage. In this manner, marriage proposals from men who are not known to the women are likely to be turned down.

It is not surprising for a lady to accept a marriage proposal from a man she does not know—this has been tradition! Due to their agreements, the father of the bride will ask for the bride wealth payment from the son-in-law. Above all, it is important to know that the bride has the final say regarding her marriage. After she agrees to marry him, they become husband and wife. Their marriage is legitimate. Most of the Anuak marriages are conducted in their own settings: Although there are witnesses present, there are no marriage certificates from courts or churches! It is a woman's agreement to get married and her parents' approval that makes it legitimate.

Biel is when a father gives his daughter to someone who can afford a full bride wealth, or in other words it is an arranged marriage. As a rule, a selected husband is always capable of paying the bride-wealth requested by his father-in-law. Biel is the least popular marriage in Anuak because it is against the will of the bride. Biel occurs for various reasons. For example, a brother is about to be married, but could not afford to pay the bride price. To fulfil his marriage requirement, he would arrange his sister's marriage to a man who has bride wealth. Biel means a man gives his sister or daughter to a rich man in exchange for bride-wealth. In this arrangement, a rich man pays bride-wealth to the father of the bride. After payment is made, the bridegroom becomes a legitimate husband for that woman. Hence, **Biel** is different from **Cood** and **Nywom**. Biel does not allow girls to reject their arranged marriages!

An Anuak proverb says: "Bielalang means that the arranged marriage is a slavery"— it is a forced marriage. According to Anuak women, without the chance to develop a relationship means no love or personal connection between the arranged couple. Yet, they are entering into a partnership because of economic hardship. The arranged marriage brings an old man and a younger woman together as a husband and wife. A critical analysis of arranged marriages shows that women are unhappy in Biel marriages. Most of the women cited that their husbands are much older than them. Age gaps combined with lack of freedom for women to choose their life partners make Biel unpopular.

Some arranged marriages are made when girls are young. It deprives them the opportunity to date or choose their own husbands when they grow up because arranged marriages were made before their maturity. Some women fall into Biel marriage without fault of their own but because of the condition of their family. To illustrate this, Akwata Omot is a beautiful woman. She dated Ojulu Obang for two years. Both were in love. Akwata became pregnant with Ojulu's baby. At the beginning, Akwata and her boyfriend had a good relationship. They loved each other. After she became pregnant, Ojulu refused to marry her. Meanwhile, Akwata's older brother, Cham Omot was dating someone. He was preparing to marry his girlfriend. Cham gave the responsibility for bride-wealth to his father, Omot Gillo. In this situation, Omot was caught unprepared. He had planned that when Cham married, he would use the bride-wealth of his daughter to pay for her brother's bride-wealth. Things didn't happen as planned. The only option for him was to find a husband for his daughter. She was in a predicament! Had her boyfriend, who was the father of her child, married her, things would have been easier. The bride-wealth paid by Akwata's husband would have covered Cham's marriage. But due to her broken relationship, her father needed to arrange her marriage to someone who could pay the bride-wealth. Finally, Akwata Omot was given to Oman Opiew through an arranged marriage. "My family will look for a rich man, they will take me to the man who has bride-wealth. In most cases, women live unhappily, and in severe cases they may attempt to take their own lives," Awilli said.

Another example is Ariet Okello, a sixteen-year-old girl, who was her mother's first child. At the same time, her father Okello had older daughters who were married already. Her father had two unmarried brothers. When his first daughter was married, he gave bride-wealth to his younger brother. When his second daughter was married, Okello used that bride-wealth to marry another wife for himself. Now his youngest brother impregnated a girl and as the older brother in the family, Okello was responsible to pay bride-wealth for the girl his brother impregnated. As a result, Ariet, the sixteen-year-old girl, ended up in an arranged marriage to pay for her uncle's marriage! In Anuak culture, paying bride-wealth is the only way to legitimize marriage.

Bride Wealth: Kany

Bride-wealth is culturally accepted for all forms of marriages: Cood, Nywom, and Biel. The cost of marriage is known to everyone who lives in Anuak society. Thus, when a man plans to get married, he prepares bride-wealth for the marriage to be approved or accepted. Ironically, men who do not have bride-wealth are not allowed to marry. This is one of the obstacles for an Anuak man who wants to marry his girlfriend but does not have bride-wealth to pay the in-laws. Failure to pay the required bride-wealth leads to marriage cancellation and nullification! To save their marriage, some men will give their daughters or sisters to a wealthy man in exchange for bride wealth. This is usually a last resort after the family have tried everything without success. The bride-wealth payment begins after the families agree to the marriage.

The initial bride-wealth payment starts with **Ojiey**, an acceptance gift to the bride's father. Acceptance gifts can be a goat, sheep, cow or an amount of money. Ojiey is non-refundable and it does not count towards the bride-wealth payments either. It is used as an icebreaker between the two families to talk about the marriage. An approval of marriage is the most important step for both families: Nywom brings the two families together and the bride wealth payment comes later after the agreement has been made. The bride-wealth payment comes in different forms: Dimuy (a string of beads) is the main bride-wealth in marriage settlement. Additional payments are cows, goats, sheep, and money. In some Anuak regions, money is the main bride-wealth while the majority of the Anuaks use Dimuy as the main payment.

Wife Inheritance: Dongo-Pac

A woman who has lost her husband cohabitates with a brother of her deceased husband or stepbrother. It is culturally acceptable for the Anuak man to live with the widow. It is called Dongo-Pac in Anuak language. Therefore, Dongo-Pac, or wife inheritance, is another form of arranged marriage that takes place between a widow and a brother of her late husband. According to Luo tradition, usually, a will of the deceased husband dictates who should live with the widow after his death! Based on the will, the deceased man allows his wife to live with his brother as a married couple. Overall, cohabitation is used to maintain unity within the family of the deceased and to ensure that the widow and any children are provided for and protected.

Nearly every married man communicates the fate of his family in his will, which includes division of wealth and properties. For instance, a father had two sons, Omot and Ojulu. When he died, he had a childbearing wife. In his will, he appointed Omot to take care of his younger wife, who in this case is his young stepmother and their child. A final message from the deceased is highly honoured in Anuak culture. It is believed that the will of a dead person will never be changed by a living human. In the case of a man who died and did not have grown children, he would appoint his brother or stepbrother to take care of his family. In some cases, where the deceased person did not leave a will, his full brother takes responsibility. Sometimes if the brother is too young to cohabitate with the widow, a stepbrother would be the legitimate candidate for her. This responsibility gives valid reasons for the heir to sire children with the widow when they cohabitate! The first child born in this relationship is called **Achalla**, if it is a girl, or if it is a boy, it is called **Ochalla**. The word **Challa** refers to the time of mourning when a woman lost her husband. In this case, Achalla or Ochalla were fathered on behalf of the deceased father, who is the true husband of the widow.

Regardless of who cohabitates with the widow, they live together as a married couple and as a united family, which is number one priority in Anuak society. Maintaining family bonds is a core value that brings children who lost their fathers into their paternal family. While the widow is a young woman, life goes on with another man who is related to her late husband. Often one of the relatives of her late husband cohabitates with the widow. It is acceptable when a woman decides to stay and have children with her brother-in-law. Co-habitation happens through the woman's willingness with some widows choosing to remarry someone else from a different family when their husbands die. Hence this gives more freedom than Biel marriage.

Bride-Wealth in Anuaks Marriages

The usefulness of bride-wealth shows that Anuak marriage requires some form of payments for legitimacy and acceptance. In other parts of the world, it is the woman who is required to pay a dowry to the groom's family. However, for the Anuak people, it is the man that pays bride-wealth. This is not considered as buying a woman, but rather as a symbolic gesture to the woman's family. It is an acknowledgment of her importance in the form of compensation to the bride's family for the loss of her labour in their house. As an unmarried woman, she does a lot of things for her parents. She helps her mother with cooking, cleaning, pounding grain, serving food, winnowing, harvesting, and planting seeds in the farms, just to mention a few duties. Anuak women are hardworking! They are known for pounding white flour, cleanliness and making the best beer (kongo). Luo people in general do not like dirty people or people with poor hygiene. Anuak women not only work at home, but they also take other responsibilities outside of the home. In the time of planting crops and harvesting, women assist men in the farms to finish work that requires a collective effort to complete the job on time.

Because of the great contribution that a woman will do in her new home with her husband, the Anuak society decided to pay bride-wealth to the bride's father. Paying the bride-wealth enables the father-in-law to marry another wife to replace his daughter's labour. For example, Ajulu Omot married Cham Obang. Ajulu is a hard worker and she has been helping her mother with many chores at home. After she was married, Ajulu left her parents to live with her husband in another village far from them. She is no longer able to do the things that she was doing for her parents. So, the Anuak marriage institution requires husbands to pay bride-wealth to their fathers-in-law.

When the bride has children, the children belong to her husband's family. Hence, the father of the bride not only loses his daughter, but he also loses access to her children. This is another reason for paying bride-wealth! At the same time, bride-wealth payment gives fathers full rights to their biological children.

An Anuak lady wears traditional attire to show her culture:

The Importance of The Wedding Celebration

A wedding ceremony is one of the biggest celebrations that takes place in Anuak culture. As a reminder, most Anuak women are free to choose their partners. Lienhardt (1957, p. 351) observed a traditional wedding and he concluded that Anuak married women exercised a great deal of power over their husbands, while unmarried girls were extremely capricious and difficult with their lovers during courtships. "To court a girl is a very exacting matter for an Anuak—far more exacting than in Dinka or Nuer custom," Lienhardt said. Moreover, when a new wife is brought to her husband's home, young men must go to the house of the bride's family. Those men give presents to the bride before she agrees to leave her parent's house, and to drink water in a new house where she will stay (Lienhardt, 1957). Weddings are an honour for the new couple to live together. It is also vital for the parents of the bride to witness their daughter leaving their house happily to live with her husband. In the same manner, the bridegroom's family welcomes a new wife to their family and clan. After their wedding is completed, the young couple live close to the parents of the husband. But they live in their own house. Furthermore, Anuak couples live together only after their wedding is finalised. Even though husband and wife are married, it is still disrespectful to live together before their wedding.

With migration to the Western world, some Anuak families in the Western countries live together while they are preparing for their wedding. It is the biggest honour for a woman to have her wedding. For Anuak women, it shows genuine love, care and respect. On the other hand, the husband is proud to bring his wife home, with big celebrations of dancing and drinking! The wedding ceremony is a reminder of their journey, the beginning of their relationship, their friendship and finally the happy union. It is a sign of honour and commitment, which they make to one another.

Divorce in Anuak Society

Divorce does occur if there is incompatibility in a marriage. An arranged marriage is more likely to end in divorce than other forms of marriages because the woman did not have an opportunity to marry the man of her choice. In other forms of marriage such as Nywom and Cood, divorce rarely happens. It befalls when married couples do not get along for reasons known to them. A healthy marriage is full of love, joy, happiness, mutual understanding and planning family life together. A husband is the head of the family and he creates a conducive environment in his home through good communication with his wife. In Anuak culture, women are responsible for most things in the house. However, men hunt, fish, farm, fight in wars and are the protectors of the house or village. Lasting marriage carries emotional support and better understanding between husband and wife. Couples spend quality time together to address family's issues that may affect their marriage. It indicates that couples who act to resolve their marital issues have a better chance to maintain their marriage. Unfortunately, when marital problems are left unresolved, divorce can be the path couples choose to free themselves from dysfunctional marriages.

Since couples do not live together before marriage, it is tricky to know the true personality or attitude of a prospective partner. In most relationships, people present their positive sides in the beginning, then later in marriage, reality shows up. This sometimes comes as a shock to the newly married couple when trouble arise. These intolerable behaviours could be heavy drinking, domestic violence, cheating or lack of responsibility. These are a few reasons cited by divorcees! Consequently, they decide to dissolve their marriage and start a new life.

There are rules for the dissolution of Anuak marriages. First, divorce that involves children is different from the divorce without children. When a divorced woman has children with her former husband, there is no need to withdraw bride-wealth because of the children he fathered. In some situations, the ex-husband demands his bride-wealth back regardless of children. In this case, the father will lose parental rights of his children if he withdraws the bride-wealth that he previously paid. Let us say, Ariet married Obang. They have three children together and later they divorced. Obang decided to withdraw his bride-wealth because he needed it for his future marriage. The divorce settlement between the former husband and wife would be made before the final dissolution of the marriage. The meeting addresses the parental rights if a former husband does not withdraw his bride-wealth. But if Obang needed his bride-wealth to be paid back to him, he loses parental rights of his children. However, when a father does not withdraw his payment after divorce, he maintains parental rights of his children. This decision keeps the rights of children with their biological fathers.

On the other hand, divorce without children demands bride-wealth repayment to the former husband. The main-bride wealth will be returned to the former husband, while the acceptance gifts are non-refundable. For example, if a woman is leaving her husband for another man, the bride-wealth paid by the new husband will be used by the father of the bride to pay back the former husband. The return of the bride-wealth is done in a respectful manner that does not create conflict between the divorced couple's families.

Rights of Children of Unmarried Parents

A biological father loses his parental rights of the child if he fails to fulfill marriage requirements. For instance, a young man who impregnates a woman but never pays bride-wealth to claim his child, automatically loses his parental rights. First and foremost, bride-wealth payment is used to legitimise marriage. It also gives the biological father's authority over his children, according to Anuak culture. In this case, claiming a biological child requires bride-wealth payments by the father. For the father who does not pay bride-wealth, he is considered a sperm donor, not a father! Consequently, he cannot claim his child even though he is the biological father. A new husband, who pays bride-wealth to legitimise their marriage, becomes the father of that child. Paying the bride-wealth legitimises the stepfather in the life of the child. Together, the stepfather and his wife will raise children from her previous marriage.

In some rare situations, sons may decide to go back to their biological fathers when they grow up, which they are free to do. When this happens, a grandfather or maternal uncle will demand bride-wealth payment for the son who returned to his biological father. His uncle will ask the biological father to pay bride-wealth for his son. Hence, when a man makes his girlfriend pregnant without legitimising the marriage, her parents will take the responsibility of the child. If the young man decides to return to his biological father, who did not raise him, the biological father must compensate the family of his son's mother. This comes after examining the costs of bringing up the child. This is considered as compensation for the support that the biological father did not provide over the years. However, girls usually remain permanently with their stepfather and mother; they do not go to seek their biological father.

There is also complexity involved should the son go seeking his biological father because not every returning son is welcomed. The biological father may denounce the son and reject him. Another dilemma faced is that the son returns to his stepfather but is not welcomed as his actions might be considered a betrayal. If a biological father rejects his son, he will usually have no choice but to go live with his maternal uncles as it is an embarrassment to go back to their stepfathers. When he is ready for marriage, his stepfather will not be responsible for the bride-wealth because he was denounced by him. His maternal uncles will then take full responsibility for the payment of his bride-wealth.

However, only a very small percentage of sons try to return to their biological fathers; most of them choose to live permanently with their stepfathers, who have raised them from their childhood to manhood. In addition, when girls get married, their bride-wealth is paid directly to their stepfathers who raised them. Their bride-wealth enables their stepfather to marry another wife or give the bride-wealth to his sons to use for their own marriages.

Interview with Madam Awilli Okach Opir conducted on 21 May 2019: A Study of Anuaks' courtship and marriages from 1970s to 2019

Awilli was born in Sudan on 10 July 1956. She lived in Melbourne, Australia, during this interview. In examining Anuak's courtship rules for nearly five decades, she identified generational changes to the rules. According to Awilli, during her youth, it would take at least six months to one year before accepting a boyfriend or going out on a date. She said there were two rules for rejecting a suitor. The first is that the girl does not like the boy who spoke to her. In this situation, the girl warns him that she is not interested in him. He must stop pursuing her! The second rule of rejection is that the girl likes the boy very much, but she uses delay tactics to test his seriousness of his intentions. This vague decision from the Anuak girl confuses the males sometimes,

because there is no clear distinction between rejection or delay tactics. But time will tell if she is interested in dating him. In courtship, Anuak girls are free to choose their partners without pressure from anyone. Lienhardt (1957) asserted that Anuak girls are extremely capricious and difficult with their lovers at the beginning of their relationships.

Awilli states that a boy who is dating a girl must go through several trials before he is accepted. It is common notion among women and girls not to accept men immediately. Some women take time to know more about the man they are dating to determine whether they are serious about a life partner. This emphasises that even if the female has decided to accept the man, she still takes her time to know him better. For women, patience and perseverance is highly valued, and it is the key for men to unlock their hearts. After men overcome these challenges, Anuak women, if interested in a man, will then reciprocate his love and affection shown but only after an extensive period of the man doing the hard work. However, for men who are not serious in a long-term relationship, this effort will frustrate them, and they may terminate their pursuit of the woman. This delay strategy has been the most effective way for women to screen out uncommitted men before accepting them.

Generational Changes: How Did Anuaks Court in 1975?

As mentioned above, most Anuak marriages developed through courtship: Cood. Here is a better explanation of Anuak dating in the 1970s. When Awilli was a teenager, she said girls, fifteen to seventeen years old and young women in their twenties, would go to drum dancing in the royal court and teenage boys and young men were also there. This is the right place for boys and girls to meet! They talk to one another at the dance. This friendly environment is conducive for youths to play, talk, dance, or find someone to date. In their dating, a boy who is interested in a girl, sends his friend to act as the spokesman and to call the girl for him. The friend goes to the girl's home and calls her to come outside. The spokesman waits patiently in the compound of the girl's house until she comes to talk to him. The spokesman delivers his friend's message. The girl would say she is not feeling well, and she cannot go anywhere. The spokesman will keep coming several times. He will call her again and stand around waiting for her. If the spokesperson manages to convince the girl to meet with the potential date, they will arrange an appropriate time. Anuak boys have their own houses where they sleep. This is the place where girls meet them. The girl tells the spokesman she will come to see them. It is the rule for Anuak girls not to go to a strange man alone she always has a companion with her!

This companion becomes her spokeswoman. Before the ladies arrive, the men prepare to receive the girls. Upon their arrival, the girls are politely welcomed. They sit down—girls sit on one side, while boys sit opposite, facing them. Additionally, the boys offer tobacco and smoking pipe in case their guests' smoke. This was the respectful manner of Anuaks dating more than forty years ago! The boys always start the conversation, especially the spokesman. During their respectful conversations, each spokesperson talks on behalf of their friend.

The time from the first initial communication to the relationship developing can take between six and twelve months, according to Awilli. There is no rush to intimacy! Getting to know each other better through face-to-face communication is a panacea for a lasting relationship. If a young man passes all the tests, the young woman will commit to the relationship, but only after she eliminated any doubts she may have. Note, women's rules for dating are meant to reject men they do not like right away. Special time is reserved for the man who the lady thinks has potential! Before giving necklace beads as a confirmation of her commitment in the relationship, some ladies seek advice from their uncle's wives or their stepmothers. Awilli said, "a girl tells her uncle's wife that somebody is interested in marrying her. She gives a little background about her potential husband."

A consultation with the uncle's wife can be helpful, according to Awilli. In broad daylight, the suitor and his friend ask the lady for the beads. By giving a necklace that symbolises love and acceptance, the man becomes her sweetheart. At this time, they are boyfriend and girlfriend with a plan to marry if everything goes well in the near future. The girl offers a symbol of acceptance to the one she has fallen in love with. First, she gives him **Cang-Caa**, a bracelet made of beads and a necklace afterwards. During this time, their relationship grows stronger and they may proceed to marriage.

As youths meet at social events, it is not surprising to know who is dating who. For example, a girl who has given a necklace to her boyfriend as a sign of her commitment will usually tell her friends about it. When rumours start to circulate around the village, members of the girl's family will hear the same rumours. Meanwhile at drum dancing, her brothers and relatives are also present in the same court. In Anuak tradition, when a girl has reached maturity, her parents have the right to know who is dating her. Nevertheless, before her family makes that decision, they might have heard about their daughter's boyfriend.

Conclusion

This book provides a detailed account of how the Anuak people in South Sudan defeated British in 1912. The British forces were annihilated in the battlefield of Juom. After the first defeat in Adongo region, British tried to penetrate through Nyikani region, but there was no soft landing for them anywhere in the country. Due to the military defeat, the Anuaks were not subdued by the British in Africa during the colonial era.

Unsung Giants depicts the fascinating history of the Anuak people from ancient times to the formation of the current-day kingdom in the fifteenth century. Anuaks faced many challenges before and after contact with the British. In 1880, King Odiel Kwot began to purchase guns from Ethiopia! Anuak leaders armed their forces before the British arrived. The abundance of elephants, leopards and buffalo in the Thim forests enabled them to hunt big game to purchase weapons. Anuaks sold tusks and leopard skins to the Ethiopians in Gore. Due to these connections, Anuaks were able to arm themselves. Between 1870 and 1889, Europeans started to massacre defenceless Africans. By this time, Anuak people were already equipped with rifles the singular reason for the defeat of the British forces. For fifteen years (1912-1927), the British were banished from entering the Anuak kingdom. The Battle of Juom repudiates the notion that everyone on the continent was colonised by European powers. The Anuak resistance proved that African people would have prevailed during colonisation period. However, they were overpowered by the technical development of Europe and the production of machine guns. If the Africans and Europeans were equally equipped, militarily, history would be different today. For example, Ethiopians repelled the Italian invasion successfully at the Battle of Adwa in 1896. It showed that when Europeans attacked an African nation armed with rifles, they lost the war. This suggested that the use of machine guns favoured European expansion. The sophisticated weapons made Africans easy prey for European empires because most Africans relied on spears, arrows and bows. Overall, Ethiopians and Anuaks proved that colonisation was not Africans 'choice', but brutal invasions.

Africans were victims of slavery and colonisation and were exploited by foreigners who controlled the African continent. Despite these humiliations, it was astonishing for the Anuak tribe to defeat British on the battlefield. Anuaks opposed imperialism that demeaned and killed Africans in the name of 'civilising' blacks according to Europeans' norms and prejudices. Thus, Africans' bravery was buried since history books were written by the victors not the vanquished. From this book, the reader can see from the lens of the African heroes on the continent. After all, it is crucial for Africans to reclaim their victory that took place in Juom in 1912. It is worth mentioning that defeating British contradicted their invincibility in Africa: They could not stand against African people who were armed with firearms like them. This is an interesting story as it is uncommon to see the British as the underdog. The humiliation and defeat of the British by the Anuak people is unknown to most Africans and the rest of the world. Fortunately, Unsung Giants is here to revive this captivating and yet intricate history of the unsung African heroes who defeated the British and remained free from injustice, slavery, and colonization.

The Anuak kingdom was one the most powerful nations in Africa during the time of colonisation. It had well-armed forces carrying rifles thirty years before the British attempted to invade the kingdom. Anuak people lived in an independent state which rejected British colonisation. They valued freedom and justice in their country. For that reason, Anuaks opposed British colonisation in their country. There was no room for British brutality. They anticipated injustice and humiliation of Africans during the colonial period. Anuaks knew that African people under British rule would suffer from brutality, injustice, or involuntary service. Consequently, the Anuak people fought against the British invasion to avoid mistreatment. According to Anuaks, freedom and justice were inalienable rights that could not be taken away from them. It is their dignity as humans. Even though the British boasted of their military capability in Africa, Anuak forces defeated them. Many parts of the African continent faced humiliation due to colonialism and slavery. In this regard, the Anuak defeat of the British militarily, restored Blacks' dignity worldwide.

DEDICATION

This book is dedicated to my mother, who raised five boys as a widow. She taught me love, kindness and hard work.

To my brother, Obang, who instilled the importance of education in me, since I was in second grade.

To my lovely wife, Abang Anade Othow, who supported me from the day I planned to write this book until its completion. I am indebted to her support and encouragement which empowered me to keep writing. She took on the huge responsibility in the family, to support me and our son, Anade, for two years. As a teacher, Abang knows the importance of imparting knowledge through writing a book. Hence, the chance to learn and pass on the history of the Anuak people and their effective resistance to colonialism. I hope this book will inspire generations of readers to look at pre-colonial history through a different lens. For this reason, Abang urged me to revive the history of the Anuak people that was lost in the world history and literature. It is through her support that the Anuak unsung heroes of Africa, are recognised and their story recorded. This has led me to overcome tough challenges and turned my childhood dream of becoming a writer into reality.

ABOUT THE AUTHOR

I was born in Otalo, South Sudan, in 1978 and started primary school in Pochalla in 1990. The civil war disrupted my education and in June 1991, I went to work in the gold mines of Damballa, near Dimma, in Ethiopia. In May 1993, my older brother, Obang, returned to the family from Khartoum after more than nine years away. When Obang learnt that I was in Damballa, he immediately set out to join me. It took him five days on foot to arrive in Damballa. On 25 July, Obang and I took the seven-hour journey from the gold mines to Dimma Refugee Camp where we registered as refugees. In August 1993 at the age of 15, we enrolled in a primary and junior school in Dimma. Obang earnt a scholarship to study in Mizan High School in Ethiopia through the support of UNHCR. He graduated from high school and became an English teacher in Dimma.

After six years in the refugee camp, Obang started the refugee resettlement process to the United States and included me in the application along with his wife and son. I was granted a visa to enter the US before my brother and his family. On 3 June 1999, I left Dimma for Addis Ababa and on 15 June, travelled to the US leaving the whole family in Africa. I arrived in Fargo, North Dakota. I wrote and phoned Obang regularly, who urged me to continue my education. His words still resonate with me strongly. "If education is buried in the stone and you have no tools to break the stone, please dig it with your bare hands and get it out," Obang wrote.

My educational journey in the US started in Minneapolis, Minnesota. In September 1999, I took English as a second language (ESL) while working to support myself and family in Africa. I was just 21, in a new country, alone, but

I knew I had endured many challenges in the past and would overcome these hurdles as well. When I left the refugee camp in Ethiopia, I did not know it would be the last time to see him. Unfortunately, Obang died before he could arrive to the US. Shortly after, my mother died. Obang was my role model. He had worked to pay for his own school fees when he was just a teenager. He believed in the power of education.

I discovered the Job Corps programs that offered an adult high school diploma in Clearfield, Utah. A friend connected me with his friends in Salt Lake City. In 2002, I left my job and went to Clearfield Job Corps where I took on carpentry for vocational training. In addition, I took other classes in Adult High School to earn a high school diploma. For a year and half on campus, I completed both programs successfully! On 28 August 2003, graduated with a high school diploma from Great Basin Adult High School in Clearfield, Utah. This piece of paper gave me hope to succeed in America. After graduation, I moved to Kansas City, Missouri to attend Maplewood Community College where I graduated in 2011 with an Associate Degree. In August of the same year, I transferred to Park University to study Journalism and Political Science. Again, graduated with a bachelor's degree in 2014. I was awarded a top feature/news writer in the university and my academic achievements continued. In 2018, I graduated from Park University with a master's degree in Healthcare Administration.

ACKNOWLEDGEMENTS

As a writer, I would like to acknowledge institutions that have preserved Anuak history. Most importantly, I want to give my personal appreciation to individuals who helped me with aspects of the Anuak oral history. These individuals volunteered their time to provide a rich history of the Anuak people. Their knowledge enabled me to write the unwritten history that I hope will inspire readers to learn about the Anuaks who defeated British during colonisation in Africa. Remarkably, it is these very people whose ancestors invented the alphabet, art of writing, kingship, laws, and so forth when they were in Ancient Egypt. It was the hard work of the Anu people that built the foundation for civilisation and humanity. The Anuak people had the longest history that dated from Cuai, the Anuak prototype to Cham, the Biblical ancestors of black people. They remembered their historical roots from Cuai-Cham in ancient times. To Gillo Okwaa who founded the Anuak nation up to Ochudho, the founder of Anuak kingdom in the Upper Nile. Luos' creativity, ingenuity and political establishment of the Kush kingdom developed the world with their earliest inventions. Each leader in Anuak society added richness to their history and culture. Due to the great support of these people, I interviewed, there is now vital information written down about the Anuak legend that has been kept in people's memory. This was transmitted from one generation to another through oral communication. Therefore, I was able to translate this oral history into written form for the first time. This is a combination of oral and written history aimed to give a comprehensive history of the Anuak people. In doing so, the oral history supplements gaps and misleading information that has been omitted intentionally by some Western writers.

IN-TEXT CITATION FOR PERSONAL INTERVIEWS

(*A. Akway His Majesty King Akway,* The acquisition of firearms; The beginning of Agem, a revolution in the Anuak Kingdom. Phone interview by Okoth Opap, 6 June 2019).

(*A, Opir*, A study to examine Anuak's dating and marriages from 1970s-2019. Phone interview by Okoth Opap, 21 May 2019).

(*B, Gillo*, The Lou Nuer in Akobo? Causes of conflict between Anuak and Nuer in Akobo County. Phone interview by Okoth Opap, 23 November 2019).

(*O. Akway,* Rotation of Ocuok, a royal emblem. Phone interview by Okoth Opap, 16 May 2019).

(*O. Ojwato*, Political role of the headman of Olaw. Phone interview by Okoth Opap, 23 March 2019).

(*O. Okom,* History of the political system in Itang; Ray Gillo's military achievements in the nineteenth century. Phone interview by Okoth Opap, 27 April 2019).

REFERENCES

Collins, R. (1983). Shadows in the Grass Britain in Southern Sudan, 1918-1956.
Yale University Press, New Haven and London.

Diop, C. A. (1989). The African Origin of Civilization Myth or Reality.
HBC Publishing.

Evans-Pritchard. (1940). the Political System of the Anuak of the Anglo-Egyptian Sudan. The London School of Economics and Political Science.

Kevin, S. (2012). History of Africa, Third Edition.
Palgrave Macmillan.

Lienhardt, G. (1957, January 1). Anuak Village Headmen. Anuak Village Headmen Lienhardt, Godfrey Africa; Jan 1, 1957;27,4; Periodicals Archiev online pg. 341.

Onyala, S. (2019). A Short social and Cultural Anthropology of the Northern Luo of South Sudan. Melbourne: Printed and Bound by Lighting Source Australia.

www.ingramcontent.com/pod-product-compliance
Lightning Source LLC
Chambersburg PA
CBHW062022290426
44108CB00024B/2740